BUILD WEALTH

& Spend It All

Live The Life You Earned

STANLEY RIGGS

BUILD WEALTH & *Spend It All*
Live the Life You Earned
Stanley A. Riggs, MD
Monetary Publishing, LLC

For information about permission to reproduce selections from this book write to:

Permissions, Monetary Publishing LLC
2300 S. Dock St., Suite 105
Palmetto, FL 34221
Or visit MonetaryPublishing.com

Copyright © 2014 by Stanley A. Riggs, MD:
First Edition, 2014

Printed in the United States of America

ISBNs: 978-0-9915215-0-0 (hard cover)
        978-0-9915215-1-7 (paperback)
        978-0-9915215-2-4 (ePub)
        978-0-9915215-4-8 (mobi)
        978-0-9915215-3-1 (audio book)

LCCN 2014904861

Monetary
Publishing

Monetary Publishing LLC
2300 S. Dock St., Suite 105
Palmetto, FL 34221
MonetaryPublishing.com

Publisher's Cataloging-in-Publication
(Provided by Quality Books, Inc.)

Riggs, Stanley A.
    Build wealth & spend it all : live the life you
earned / Stanley A. Riggs, MD.
    pages cm
    Includes bibliographical references and index.
    LCCN 2014904861
    ISBN 978-09915215-0-0

    1. Finance, Personal. 2. Wealth. I. Title.
    II. Title: Build wealth and spend it all.

HG179.R54 2014   332.024
                           QBI14-600064

For Marjorie L. Riggs

My mother, whom I should have helped
to spend it all.

Table of Contents

Acknowledgments

Vicki Robin, coauthor of *Your Money or Your Life*, for permission to reproduce Figures 7-1 and 7-2.

Harry S. Dent for permission to reproduce figures 3-1 and 3-2.

Fig. 3-1 "Top 10% of Households, Income by Age" reproduced from *The Demographic Cliff*, Harry S. Dent, Penguin Group, New York, NY, 2014, p.42, with permission of Dent Research.

Fig. 3-2 "Consumer Life Cycle" reproduced from *The Demographic Cliff*, Harry S. Dent, Penguin Group, New York, NY, 2014, p.12, with permission of Dent Research.

Fig. 7-1 "The Fulfillment Curve," reproduced from *Your Money Or Your Life*, Vicki Robin and Joe Dominguez, Penguin Books, New York, NY, 2008, p. 24, with permission.

Fig. 7-2 "The Crossover Point," reproduced from *Your Money Or Your Life*, Vicki Robin and Joe Dominguez, Penguin Books, New York, NY, 2008, p. 243, with permission.

Vicki Rollo of Rollo Design for creating the illustrations.

Introduction

FAILING MY OWN MOTHER

I sat in the "nice" nursing home watching the 96-year-old, 5 foot, 85-pound shadow of my mother nod off during our conversation.

She was one of the cherished "private pay" residents. Only the accounting office—not the nursing staff or other residents—knew whose retirement savings were being automatically debited by hundreds of dollars a day and whose expenses were being paid in full by Medicaid.

But I knew. I knew they were taking the money she had earned as a first grade teacher and which my father, now deceased, had earned as a small-town municipal worker. Their savings represented their combined 90 years of work. It was money they had saved by driving secondhand cars, taking day-trip vacations and seldom choosing to dine out.

They could take money from her because she had saved it. They couldn't take money from the others because they had chosen to enjoy spending it.

I advised my mother and father how to save, when I should have advised them how to spend.

I suggested responsible investment tools, when I should have suggested responsible, enjoyable experiences.

I encouraged financial safety, when I should have encouraged enjoyable living.

xiv | BUILD WEALTH & *Spend It All*

I am guilty of having failed my mother in a horrible and unforgivable way—one that she will never know, and I will never forget.

But I will not fail myself.

During 50-plus years of building wealth, I have learned three important principles:

(1) Know the difference between assets and liabilities, and put money into the assets.

(2) Be aware of and understand the implications of the coming demographic changes.

(3) Always know where you are in the economic cycle and never forget the principal of reversion to the mean.

Over the last several years I have become aware of the threats that are facing my hard-earned savings. I hear talk about "inequality of income," but all I see is inequality of work effort. I read about the increase in the poverty rate but I also notice the dramatic decrease in the U.S. labor force participation rate. I'm concerned about our country running out of money, but I also fear for the safety of the $11 trillion sitting, untaxed, in 401(k) and IRA plans, only a few keystrokes away from being nationalized and redistributed into underfunded union and municipal pension programs in the name of "fairness." Anyone with any reasonable amount of net worth needs to give serious thought as to how they plan to keep from having their retirement savings redistributed in the not too distant future.

But just this past year, while visiting my mother in the nursing home, I came to realize that building wealth and keeping it safe is just opportunity unrealized unless until I actually convert it into "fun stuff" or meaningful gifting before it is taken away and before I die.

That is when I decided I needed a plan to responsibly and strategically spend down my entire net worth over a predetermined period of time and die broke—insolvent but not illiquid or destitute. And that's just what I did.

I decided that at the end of my life, I am willing to be in voluntarily and strategically planned, diminished circumstances...but with great memories.

I plan to be the guy in the nursing home who is broke but with rich memories, rather than rich but with broken dreams.

And, if I die doing what I love—sailing on my boat, perhaps during a storm—I will be going out of this world the same way I came into it: screaming, wet, bloody, and, of course, *broke*.

That hyphen between those two dates on your gravestone is not very long, so you need to get started now, regardless of your age.

So get on this ride, strap in and hold on, while you too learn how to build wealth, how to protect it, and how to give yourself permission to enjoy...*spending it all.*

Warning—Disclaimer

This publication is designed to provide reliable information on the subjects covered. It is sold with the understanding that the publisher and author are neither licensed for nor engaged in rendering legal, accounting or other professional services. The author is not a certified public accountant or a registered financial planner and speaks from only his personal experiences. If legal or other expert assistance is desired, the services of a competent professional, preferably one who has himself or herself attained the goals you desire, should be sought.

It is not the purpose of this book to reprint all the information that is otherwise available on these subjects. Every effort has been made to make this publication as complete and accurate as possible. However, there may be mistakes, both typographical and in content. Therefore, this material should be used only as a general guide and not as the ultimate source of information.

The financial concepts expressed here are not suitable for everyone and might not be appropriate for your specific objectives, financial situation and needs. Before making any significant financial or life-altering decision, always consult with trusted professionals and with family members who might also be affected.

The purpose of this publication is to educate, entertain and inspire. The author and publisher specifically disclaim any liability or responsibility to any person or entity with respect to any loss or damage caused, or alleged to have been caused, directly or indirectly, by the concepts or application of the contents of this book.

I am clearly an advocate of demographics and of Harry S. Dent's application of demographic data (specifically his "Spending Wave") to economic forecasting. I'm not affiliated with his organization and I receive no compensation for mentioning his books or any of the other books mentioned, referenced or recommended herein.

PART I

BUILD YOUR WEALTH

CHAPTER ONE
Understanding Assets and Liabilities

The first requirement of building wealth is to know the difference between assets and liabilities. You will never be successful in building wealth unless you have a clear understanding of the difference between an "asset" and a "liability." None of the poor and few of the middle class understand this important distinction. The wealthy not only understand the difference, but are able to exploit their understanding to their advantage.

In his book *Rich Dad, Poor Dad,* author Robert T. Kiyosaki states: "An asset is something that puts money into your pocket. A liability is something that takes money out of your pocket." [1]

Everyone has the same basic expenses of taxes, housing (mortgage or rent), utilities, food, clothing and transportation. But what separates the rich from the poor and the wealthy from the rich are their assets and liabilities.

ASSETS

Assets put money into your pocket, preferably each month. They will feed you even if you are not working. Examples of assets include:

- Income-generating real estate
- Dividend-paying stocks
- Interest-paying bonds

Consider the following remark attributed to Albert Einstein: "Compound interest is the eighth wonder of the world. He who understands it... earns it. He who doesn't... pays it."

Manhattan Island was purchased by the European colonists in 1626 for $24 worth of beads and trinkets. The Native Americans probably thought that was a deal, while the settlers thought it was a steal. But if one had invested the $24 dollars in a theoretical 388-year bond maturing in 2014 yielding 7 percent annually, the compounded interest would have a value of over $6 trillion today, more than enough to buy all of New York City, including its infrastructure and other "tenant improvements."

As an asset class, real estate has the advantage of being able to generate four types of income:

(1) Rental income
(2) Depreciation
(3) Tax advantages
(4) Appreciation

LIABILITIES

Liabilities take money out of your pocket, usually monthly. They will eat your income even if you are working. The most common liabilities are:

- Credit cards with outstanding balances
- Consumer loans
- Home equity lines of credit
- Home mortgages

That is correct: your home mortgage is actually a liability to you and an asset to the mortgage holder. Colleagues would argue with me about this, but after the 2008 home mortgage crisis, they have remained silent. Your home (mortgage, property taxes, insurance, maintenance and repair) takes money out of your pocket every 30 days, and if you were to lose your job, this liability would be the one that would eat your savings the fastest.

The home mortgage is an asset only to the bank that made the loan and holds the mortgage. The home puts money in the bank's pocket every month. As the homeowner, you just have the privilege of paying for the maintenance, insurance and property taxes on the bank's income stream.

Most poor and middle class people spend their hard-earned money on life's fixed expenses and their "stuff" (personal belongings) that goes into their Liability Box (see Figure 1-1 below). That "stuff" costs money to buy and money to maintain, and loses its original value over time. Most importantly, buying stuff keeps you from building wealth.

CALCULATING YOUR NET WORTH

Net worth is the difference between your true assets and your actual liabilities.

Assets – Liabilities = Net Worth

Many people often "pad" their net worth by inflating it artificially with personal belongings that, while having a high perceived or emotional value, carry an actual value just above junk to everybody else. These might include clothing, furniture, small boats, old motorcycles. The wealthy know what truly represents an asset or liability.

CASH FLOW OF POOR HOUSEHOLDS

Everyone has expenses. What characterizes poor households is that almost all of their earned income goes into the Expense Box (see Fig. 1-1 below). They struggle just to maintain a roof over their heads, food on the table, and a car in the driveway—if they are lucky. They have just a little money to put into their Liability Box and, of course, no money for the Asset Box. This sad domestic cash flow means they do not have many options available to them; they are basically "stuck."

Fig. 1-1 Cash Flow Path of Poor Households

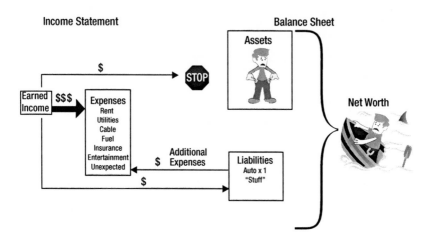

CASH FLOW OF MIDDLE CLASS AND RICH HOUSEHOLDS

That's right; I include rich households in with the middle class households because their domestic spending is similar and not at all like the domestic spending of the wealthy households.

Rich people are often characterized as having high earned incomes. But usually they also have expensive lifestyles with a lot of "stuff" in their Liability Box, sometimes to the extent that, although they are high earners, they live paycheck to paycheck. They tend to be the most visible community professionals, such as successful physicians, dentists and attorneys. Their flow of money is from the Earned Income Box down to the Liability Box and then out (Fig. 1-2).

Again, everyone has the basic daily expenses in the Expense Box, and the middle class and rich households have proportionately more daily expenses than the poor households.

But the big difference you will see in Fig. 1-2 is the huge amount of "stuff" in the Liability Box, which drains a disproportionately high percentage of the earned income to support it. The second characteristic that you will notice is that, as with the poor households, there is no money flowing into the Asset Box to generate passive income. This is a tragic domestic cash flow. Unlike the poor, the middle class and rich do have options available to them, but every time they pull out their credit card or checkbook they just keep choosing the wrong options.

Fig. 1-2 Cash Flow Path of Middle Class / "Rich" Households

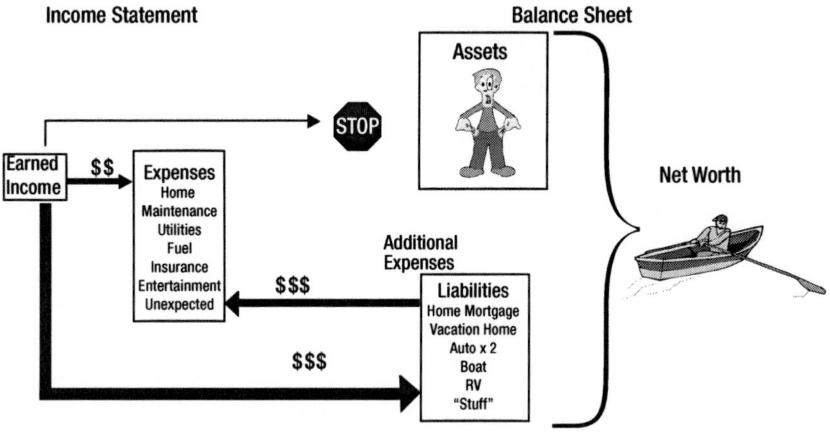

CASH FLOW OF WEALTHY HOUSEHOLDS

As you will see in Fig. 1-3, not only do wealthy households have more money flowing out of the Earned Income Box, but more importantly, they have an additional income box called the Passive Income Box.

Although this group spends more money on their Expense Box, they spend a *smaller percentage* of their earned income on expenses. And although they have more "stuff" in their Liability Box, they spend their passive income rather than their earned income supporting these liabilities. You now see a flow of earned income into the Asset Box. Unlike the poor, middle class or rich, the wealthy households have built up income generators in the Asset Box which allow income to flow back into the Passive Income Box. Cash can now flow from the Passive Income Box to support the Liability Box and, most importantly, back into the Asset Box to build new income-generating assets.

What separates the wealthy from the middle class and rich is this automatic feedback loop between the Asset Box and the Passive Income Box. At some level this feedback loop becomes self-sustaining, the Earned Income Box becomes less relevant, and the household becomes truly, independently wealthy.

This harmonious, independently wealthy lifestyle, once achieved, is not guaranteed in perpetuity. Putting some high maintenance "stuff" into the Liability Box, going through a divorce, or the untimely death of the wealth-building individual can short circuit the feedback loop and make the Earned Income Box once again the primary money generator. This is why the top 5 percent income group has an annual turnover rate of 20 percent.

Fig. 1-3 Cash Flow Path of Wealthy Households

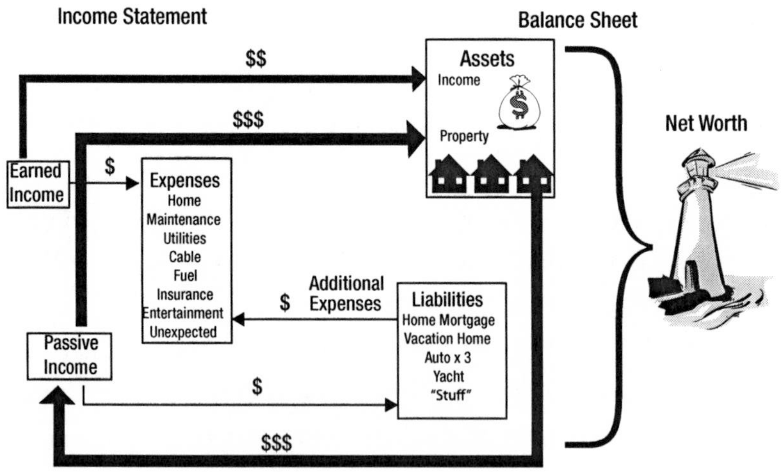

SAVING ISN'T ENOUGH

Saving money has always been the cornerstone for financial self-reliance and success. But outside of an IRA or 401(k) tax deferral plan, you are saving after-tax money—money you have worked for but only received after the local, state and federal governments have taken up to 52 percent. Outside of living a long, self-impoverished life of sacrifice, you will never be able to "save" your way to being wealthy.

Earning a pile of net worth then spending it and dying broke while elderly is very different from living a long life of self-impoverishment.

GOOD DEBT AND BAD DEBT

The "talking heads" television pundits advocate cutting up your credit cards, paying off all your debt, and never getting back into debt. Too bad it's not that simple. Staying out of debt is a good plan to avoid going broke, but it is not a plan to build wealth.

It is important to distinguish between "good debt" and "bad debt." An example of good debt is a loan on an income-producing property that is an asset, produces income and increases in value over the term of the loan.

Productive or "good debt" is self-liquidating (pays itself off) and has a passive return that significantly exceeds the borrowing costs. Ideally there is a spread of 5 percent to 15 percent between the borrowing costs (loan interest rate) and the asset's income stream (cash-on-cash, cap rate or ROI).

Bad debts are loans for unnecessary items that will go right into the Liability Box, where they can lose 20 percent of their value within the first 20 minutes of ownership. Examples include a loan to buy a boat, Jet Ski or an unnecessary, expensive vehicle. Liabilities require money (work, time and effort) to be maintained. They lose value over the term of the loan, and divert money that could otherwise be going into assets and building wealth.

In his book *Cash Flow Quadrant*, Robert Kiyosaki says: "Every time you owe somebody money, you become an employee of that money. If you take out a 30 year loan, you become a 30 year employee." [2]

OTHER PEOPLE'S MONEY (OPM) AND OTHER PEOPLE'S TIME (OPT)

To build wealth you need to judiciously use other people's money (OPM), other people's time (OPT) and unrealized, untaxed, capital gains—not just your after-tax, earned income.

The poor and middle class go through life working for earned income which becomes someone else's passive income (usually the bank shareholders' or landlord's). The wealthy have learned to turn this equation around by using someone else's earned income as their passive income by investing in income-producing assets. One example would be rental properties. Your industrial and commercial properties house small businesses whose employees and owners go to work every day to generate your cash flow to pay your mortgage, property taxes and insurance, with money left over for you to enjoy or to reinvest in other income-producing assets and build wealth. Rental homes have tenants who get up to go to work five days or more a week, with the first seven to ten working days of their month generating your rental income.

I used the terms "other people's money" (OPM) and "other people's time" (OPT) above. OPT is passive income that relies on "other people's time." It is safer to build wealth using OPT rather than OPM.

Just as there are the apparent rich who will never be truly wealthy, there are some wealthy persons—with assets that produce more money than their liabilities require—who might never appear to be rich.

This independent wealth is not just a number, but rather the relationship between available passive income and the expenses that need to be paid. One can be independently wealthy with relatively little passive income as long as the expenses are relatively low. This is addressed with two revealing diagrams in Chapter 7, "Lifestyle: You Have Choices."

Wealth is not only the measure of money but also a measure of time. Wealth is the ability of a person and his family to survive for a period of time without working. The truly wealthy can live off of their assets for the rest of their lives without working. The very wealthy can afford to donate money to charitable causes and still never run out of money because the contents of their Asset Boxes put more money into their Passive Income Boxes than the liabilities take out.

GETTING PROPER FINANCIAL ADVICE

The primary reason why so many people lose their money or fail to achieve significant wealth is because they fail to seek financial advice from successful wealthy investors. It is always better to seek advice from someone who has already arrived at a place where you aspire to be.

Stock Brokers: Always seek advice from people who have already accomplished what you are trying to achieve. For example, if you have one or two rental houses, you will want to get your real estate advice from an investor who has five or ten rental houses, not a stock broker. Remember that the stock broker is cold calling you so he can make money investing *your* portfolio—because *his* portfolio is nonexistent! Why? Because… wait… wait… here it comes… he is an unsuccessful investor! And now he wants *you* to pay *him* to tell you how to invest *your* money!

Financial Advisors: Most financial advisors provide above-average advice to average investors who have less than average expectations. The median income for financial advisors is $67,000 annually. The only reason they get out of bed, put on a suit, fight the morning traffic and listen to clients complain to them about the latest great opportunity they heard about last weekend at some cocktail party is because they do not have enough of *their own* money to invest. Most financial advisors who win $5 million in the lottery will promptly stop returning your calls. Almost any financial advisor who quits his day job today will have his car repossessed in 6 months and his house foreclosed on in year. Why? Because the vast majority never have and never will build true wealth for themselves, so don't expect them to be able to do it for you, either.

Only seek advice from someone lower than you on the financial ladder when you want to know what *not* to do with your money. Warren Buffett has famously said: "Wall Street is the only place where people arrived in Mercedes to take financial advice from people who arrived on the subway." Popular magazines sell themselves by rotating the topics on their covers to include one of the Big Three: "lose weight," "retire young and rich," and "improve your sex life." Building wealth requires knowledge, a sound plan and perseverance.

> As a preteen I worked as a golf caddy. That was back in the pre-golf cart days when someone had to carry the bag of golf clubs around the 18-hole golf course. I never made much money, but I did get a lot of advice. I watched as the golfers unloaded their golf bags from the trunks of their automobiles. I sought their advice only if they drove a Cadillac, Lincoln or Thunderbird (superficial and anecdotal but, hey, cut me some slack here; I was ten years old!). I always managed to work my question into the conversation:
> "What you do for a living?"
> The advice I most commonly heard was:
> "Get a good education, learn a skill, start your own business and work hard."
> I didn't quite understand their other advice:
> "Keep your first wife."

IT'S SIMPLE... BUT NOT EASY

To gain further insight into who the wealthy really are, consider reading the following books: *The Millionaire Mind, The Millionaire Next Door, The Richest Man in Town,* and *The Top 10 Distinctions between Millionaires and the Middle Class.* (I have referenced these books for you in the notes for Chapter 1 in the back of the book.) The theme most commonly seen in these books is that wealth is often the result of hard work, perseverance, and self-discipline. Ninety percent of today's wealth is first-generational.

There is no quick and easy way to build wealth. It is like losing weight or giving up smoking: It is simple, but not easy. Everyone knows that to lose weight you just stop putting calories in your mouth. To quit smoking, you just stop lighting cigarettes. It is not a mystery. It's simple... but not easy.

YOU NEED A PLAN

Building wealth requires both hard work and a viable plan. The work effort involves getting up when others are sleeping, working while others are playing, and still working while others are watching TV or after they have gone to bed. That's why it's called "work."

You also need a plan to put your hard-earned money into something that will put money into your pocket each month and not into something that will just eat a hole in your pocket. That is why it is critical to understand the difference between an "asset" and a "liability" and to put your hard hard-earned money into the assets.

WORK VS. HOBBY

If you want to make enough money to not only support yourself and your family at the standard of living to which you aspire, but also to put into real assets to build wealth, you will need to actually do "work." Whether or not you enjoy it is irrelevant. That is why they call it "work" and not "play." If everyone thought your job was fun, you would have to buy a ticket and wait in line with everyone else to do it. You would not be getting paid to do it. It's work. Get over it. Move on.

If what you do results in a lot of satisfaction but not enough pay to support your desired lifestyle, you have a hobby, not a real, adult job. Your parents might have told you to "find something you like to do" for a living. But if what you like to do involves playing the guitar for a living or painting portraits, you will never be able to build wealth unless you become a rock star.

Likewise, your parents might have told you as a child that you could do anything you put your mind to. They lied. No amount of positive thinking or wishful desire can make you something you are not. If that were the case, I would be playing first base for the Boston Red Sox instead of writing this book. You must be able to make an honest assessment of your abilities and talents.

It is necessary to learn a skill that will give the people out in the real world a reason to pay you. The best and hardest working car valet in town is not going to be able to work hard or long enough to earn as much money as the laziest, dumbest attorney in town. Interviews with the wealthy have revealed not only the need to work hard, but also the need to work hard at an endeavor that has the potential to be prosperous. As Warren Buffett says: "It's financially better to be mediocre in a great business than to be great in a mediocre business." So part of your plan should be to pick a field where you are well compensated for your time and efforts.

When I was a child my parents put a framed quote on my bedroom wall:

Press On

"Nothing in the world can take
the place of persistence.
Talent will not; nothing is more common
than unsuccessful men with talent.
Genius will not; unrewarded genius
is almost a proverb.
Education will not; the world is
full of educated derelicts.
Persistence and determination alone are omnipotent.
The slogan 'Press On!' has solved and always
will solve the problems of the human race."

— President Calvin Coolidge

My mother was a first grade teacher, and she must have realized early on that it was my sister who got the brains. If there was to be any hope for me, I would need to learn persistence and determination.

SMALL BUSINESS = JOB OWNERS

Be aware that most small business owners actually own a job and not a business.

If you need to turn the key in the lock every morning to make money, you own a job and not a business.

If you cannot go out of town without losing money or needing to remain in daily contact with the business, you own a job and not a business.

If you are the first to take a pay cut and the last to be paid, you own a job and not a business.

In the end, most small, pseudo-businesses end up having no value, or the only asset they have to sell after many years of operation is their building—if they own it. The lesson here is that you want to own the property or the building in which the small businesses operate. Let them risk their life savings and put their time and effort into paying you the rent. Small businesses, one after another, will cycle through your properties, paying your mortgage, your property taxes, and your insurance, and building your wealth while they run their hobbies and lose their savings.

It is often said that the main difference between a rich person and a poor person is what they do in their spare time. I would qualify that with "what they have done *during* their spare time in their life."

It is never too late in life for those with the motivation to start to build wealth. Kentucky Fried Chicken founder Harland Sanders began building his wealth late in life. His successful roadside restaurant (pre-KFC) was bypassed by an interstate highway and he suddenly found himself broke at age 65, collecting Social Security and holding a secret recipe for fried chicken. He started over by working out of the trunk of his car.

W. Randall Jones, founder of *Worth* magazine states there are three types of people [3]:

- ▸ Those who make things happen
- ▸ Those who watch things happen
- ▸ Those who have no idea what is happening

Personal responsibility is the true path to both financial and personal success. Success is a choice… it's **your** choice.

SUMMARY

Building wealth is like losing weight or quitting smoking. It is simple, but not easy.

Both demographic studies and popular books about millionaires all arrive at the same conclusion: wealth is most often the result of hard work, perseverance and self-discipline. It requires both responsibility and accountability.

The first requirement for building wealth is to know the difference between an asset and a liability and to put your money into assets. An asset will put money into your pocket, preferably monthly, and a liability will take money out of your pocket, probably monthly.

You need to have a skill that enables you to perform a task for which someone else is willing to pay you. Doing something you like to do is called a hobby. Building wealth requires real work. You are not required to enjoy it.

You need a plan. Most small business owners just own a job, not a business. You don't want to own the small business. You want to own the building the small business operates in or the rental houses the employees live in. Let someone else risk their life savings and work six days a week to earn the money to pay your mortgage, your property taxes and your insurance—with enough left over to help you to build your own wealth.

Always seek financial advice from those who are higher up on the financial food chain. It's better to get advice from someone who has already accomplished what you are attempting to achieve.

In addition to a clear understanding of assets and liabilities, it is critical to know how to anticipate, identify and avoid short-term financial disasters by understanding economic cycles (Chapter 2) and long-term financial dead ends by understanding the effects of demographic changes (Chapter 3).

CHAPTER TWO
Understanding Economic Cycles

It is not the strongest or the most intelligent of the species that survive, but the ones most responsive to change.
— Charles Darwin

Financial opportunities are always recurring and are always present somewhere. When either people or markets make mistakes, often exceptional opportunities arise.

Economic cycles, often referred to as "booms" and "busts," have been around as long as mankind has been trading goods. The first boom was perhaps the first unexpectedly productive garden and the first bust perhaps the first unusually cold winter that followed.

In the industrialized world of the 18th and 19th centuries, these regularly occurring economic cycles were extreme and they had catastrophic consequences in the days before safety nets. They always climax with human folly and the utterance of "It's different this time."

It is commonly said in the business world that the Chinese Sino-character for "crisis" is a combination of two characters: one meaning "danger" and the other meaning "opportunity" (actually not true, and the Chinese really hate hearing that). But the point is that where there is a crisis there is usually an opportunity. Understanding economic cycles will help you to not only avoid the dire consequences of human folly, but to position yourself to actually benefit from it. It is not immoral to benefit from a crisis as long as you are not the one who causes it (e.g., Wall Street).

SKATE TO WHERE THE PUCK *IS GOING*

Wayne Gretzky, considered to be one of the greatest hockey players of all time, is often quoted as saying "I skated to where the puck was going, not where it was."

By understanding and following economic cycles you will always be able to skate to, or invest in, where the puck is going and not, like the herd, to where it is or where it has already been.

GREED + STUPIDITY = OPPORTUNITY

Historical Context

Isaac Newton, while Master of the Mint in 1720, stated: "I can calculate the motions of the heavenly bodies, but not the madness of people." Newton was a hapless speculator who doubled his money investing in the South Sea Company. He reinvested to "double down" on his winnings, only to lose most of his wealth.

In his book *One Hundred Years of Land Values in Chicago: The Relationship of the Growth of Chicago to the Rise of Its Land Values, 1830–1933* (University of Chicago Press, 1933), Homer Hoyt catalogued the five boom and bust cycles of real estate prices in Chicago. From this and other writings, we can see that the 2008 U.S. housing crisis was not a "Black Swan" or an unpredictable event. It was just another cycle whose long duration made it difficult to put into perspective unless one is familiar with historical data.

In *Financial Crises and Periods of Industrial and Commercial Depression* published in 1902, author Theodore E. Burton states: "When these disturbances occur, committees of Congress or Parliament are appointed to investigate. These committees take testimony and collect voluminous information from many sources. In all the testimony there is an evident exaggeration of the efficiency of law and of government action redeeming the difficulty." [1]

This sounds so much like the 2009–2012 congressional hearings about who was to blame and what regulations (such as the Dodd-Frank Act) are needed to prevent a recurrence.

It was Thomas Robert Malthus (1798) who developed one of the best models of economic cycles, earning economics the label "Dismal Science" because of his use of economics with the dire prediction about the future and Britain's eventual mass poverty and stagnation.

In his book *Money, Bank Credit, and Economic Cycles*, Jesus Huerta de Soto states: "With the Napoleonic Wars, the start of the Industrial Revolution and the spread of the fractional-reserve banking system, business cycles began to reappear with great regularity and acquired the most significant typical features." [2]

The Panic of 1819 particularly affected the United States. The panic was preceded by an expansion of credit and the money supply, both in the form of bank bills and loans. The newly created Bank of the United States played a leading role in the process. This U.S. Central Bank produced an artificial economic expansion which was suddenly interrupted in 1819 when the bank ceased to expand credit.

The 1896 credit expansion for the "new" investment opportunities of electric power, telephone and shipbuilding (replacing the prior over-investment darling: railroads) set the stage for the severe 1907 banking crisis and severe recession. This is not unlike the recent housing boom and subsequent bust fueled by artificially low interest rates.

ASSET BUBBLES

It has been said that our human tendencies cause us to perceive a low risk near market peaks, when the risk is highest, and high risk at market bottoms, when it is lowest. These are "asset bubbles." Robert J. Shiller of Yale University describes an asset bubble as "... a psycho-economic phenomena. It's like a mental illness. It is marked by excessive enthusiasm, participation of the news media and feelings of regret among people who were in the bubble." [3]

Technically, an asset bubble is an increase in the price of an asset of more than two standard deviations above the trend, taking inflation into account. Using this standard, there have been over 300 asset bubbles between 1720 and 2010. See Appendix 3: "Famous Bubbles in History" for a list of the most common economic bubbles in history.

POPULAR ECONOMIC CYCLES

Here are a few well-known economic cycles. After reading this list, you will understand why some economic cycles might be considered to be dubious at best.

- ▸ Kondratiev (Nikolai) or K-Wave Cycle, lasting 45–60 years.
- ▸ Elliott Wave, with 8 components, popularized by Robert Prechter (2002).
- ▸ Juglar Cycle (Clement Juglar), lasting between 7 and 11 Years, Popularized by Joseph Schumpeter and having 4 periods: (1) expansion, (2) crisis, (3) recession, (4) recovery. This seems to closely describe the U.S. real estate cycles.
- ▸ Sunspot Cycles, occurring every 11 years based on the recurrence of "small" (the size of planet Earth) cooler, dark spots on the sun (not solar flares), first observed in 325 BC and recorded on a regular basis since the 17th century.

What should you get out of this list? Just understand that economic cycles do exist. When times are bad, prepare for a change for the better, and when times are great, brace for a change for the worse. And remember to *skate to where the puck is going.* It is not as complicated as some would like to make it out to be.

LINEAR THOUGHT

The most common mistake even the so-called pros make is to apply linear thought to nonlinear, cyclical events. When the stock market was booming in 1999, the linear thinkers were talking about the "new metrics" and they extrapolated out the cyclical curve to a linear, climbing forecast. When even the waitresses at IHOP were making money flipping houses in 2007, the mortgage brokers were talking about the "new paradigm" as they too extrapolated out the cyclical curve to an endless, linear, climbing forecast. Even at the bottom of the Great Recession, in March 2009, Wall Street sage and PIMCO bond fund managing director Mohamed El-Erian coined the phrase "the new normal," implying a lack of economic recovery as he employed linear thought to extrapolate out the cyclical recovery curve to almost a flat line.

HORRIBLY WRONG PREDICTIONS

In his book, *Conquer The Crash*, Robert Prechter (2002) states: "Two years ago, (2000) as most major U.S. stock indices reached their all-time highs, the Wall Street Journal observed 'economists are downright euphoric.' Of the 50 economists surveyed, all but two were bullish for 2000. One year later, when the DOW, S & P 500, and NASDAQ were down 8 percent, 15 percent and 51 percent from their respective highs and the onset of the recession was just weeks away, the consensus for continued growth was even stronger. Only one economist out of 54 surveyed call for a recession in 2001." [4]

In the 2008 stock market meltdown, Warren Buffet's Berkshire Hathaway lost 33 percent of its stock value and both the Harvard and Yale University endowment funds lost over 20 percent of their values. Nobody's right all the time.

One of the most famous bad stock market predictions was made by Irving Fisher, inventor of the Rolodex file system. Just a few days prior to the 1929 stock market crash, the Yale economics professor proclaimed support for the U.S. stock market values and subsequently lost his entire personal fortune and his academic reputation.

The economist Kenneth Galbraith (WSJ, January 22, 1993) wrote "There are two kinds of forecasters: those who don't know and those who don't know they don't know." This brings up the old joke about economists:

Question: "Why did God make economists?"

Answer: "To make weathermen look good."

See the Chapter Notes section for some examples with book titles claiming Dow 30,000, Dow 36,000, Dow 40,000, and Dow 100,000. I read these and other incorrect economic predictions to do what I call "forensic" or "autopsy" reading. Understanding why a false prediction was wrong can be just as instructive as understanding why a true prediction was correct.

TOOLS FOR ANTICIPATING ECONOMIC CYCLES

There are always investment opportunities.

During the Great Depression (1929–1932), the stock market fell 89 percent, but you could have been spared by investing in the long-term government bonds which increased 14 percent, one-year government notes which increased 12 percent, long-term corporate bonds which increased 9 percent, or treasury bills which increased 5 percent during that same time period.

Famous economists such as Keynes, Hayek, Minsky, Friedman and others—although having different economic theories—agreed that a capitalist economy is far too complex for anyone to be sure that any one model is better than another, especially when it comes to predicting future events.

The following four indicators are reliable and will help you to follow economic cycles:

- ▶ Composite Index of Leading Economic Indicators
- ▶ Yield Curve
- ▶ Institute of Supply Management (ISM)
- ▶ Chicago Board Options Exchange Market Volatility Index (VIX)

For the short-term perspective, use the Leading Economic Indicators, Yield Curve, the latest ISM figures, and real-time VIX. These indicators are described in the following pages and are readily available online and should be reviewed weekly.

For the long-range, broad perspective, use the demographic Spending Wave model discussed further in Chapter 3 "Understanding Demographics." This should be reviewed semi-annually.

Composite Index of Leading Economic Indicators

This data is released from the U.S. Commerce Department. From 1959–2001 it forecasted all seven recessions that did occur and five recessions that did not occur.

Yield Curve

The most accurate economic indicator has proven to be the yield curve—the plotted range of yields of U.S. treasuries from short- to long-term maturities. There is a strong correlation between this interest rate spread and the future U.S. GDP, six to twelve months ahead. This tool has proven to have the highest success rate for forecasting the inflection points in U.S. business activity.

A slightly rising yield curve, as shown in Fig. 2-1, is thought to be ideal. A steeply climbing curve (Fig. 2-2) illustrates long-term

U.S. Treasury rates significantly higher than short-term rates; this is a forecast for economic growth. A flat yield curve (Fig. 2-3) is indicative of a possible recession. An inverted or downward curve illustrating long-term rates lower than short-term rates, illustrated in Fig. 2-4, indicates the probability of an economic downturn. Since 1960, all seven U.S. recessions have been preceded by inverted yield curve months in advance. The 3 month/30-year rate spread averages 2.5 percentage points.

The recent Federal Reserve manipulation of the markets through its Quantitative Easing policy of expanding the monetary base by $85 billion a month for over four years might prove to skew this otherwise reliable indicator.

Fig. 2-1 Normal Yield Curve

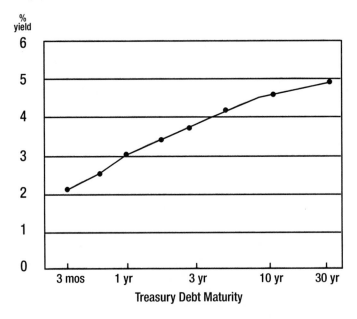

Fig. 2-2 Steep Yield Curve – Growth Ahead

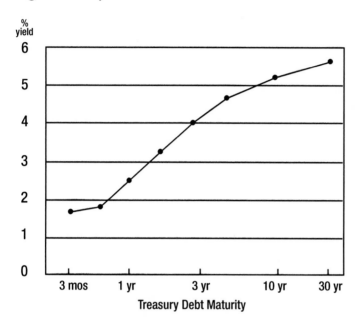

Fig. 2-3 Flat Yield Curve – Recession Possible

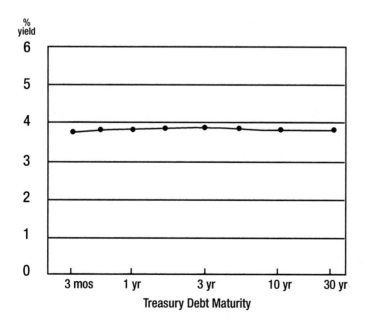

Fig. 2-4 Inverted Yield Curve – Recession Unavoidable

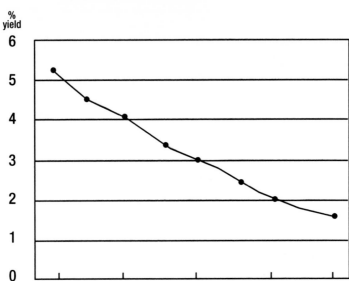

Institute of Supply Management (ISM)

The Institute of Supply Management is a private institute founded in 1915. They release to the public monthly reports on the recent trends of purchasing and supply management professionals. These trends have implications on future economic activity. This privately generated data is thought by some to be more accurate and reliable than the government-supplied data.

Chicago Board Options Exchange Market Volatility Index (VIX)

This index, which has been around since 1986, is a measure of the implied volatility of the Standard and Poor (S+P 500) index based on options and future trades. If your financial advisor thinks the "VIX" is a brand of cough drops, you've got a problem.

REVERSION TO THE MEAN

Reversion to the mean is a concept, that when correctly applied to a cyclical (not a life cycle) situation, assumes that both the highs and the lows are only temporary, and values will always move back to the mean or average as they over-correct and continue on to the next high or low inflection point.

The biggest mistake even the economists make is to consider the values as reverting only *back to the mean*. If that were the case, the mean would constantly be changing. In reality, the values revert back to the mean and *continue to overshoot the mean* before reaching their next high or low inflection point. It is the constant, symmetrical, bi-directional overshooting of the mean value that keeps the mean or average value stable.

For example, if you are wondering where interest rates will go next, just consider where the rates currently are in respect to their mean. This reversion to, and then beyond, the mean, only applies to cyclical and not life cycle models.

Example: 10-year treasury rates
    Low – 1.91 January 2013
          1.95 January 1941
    High – 14.59 January 1982
    Mean – 6.6 percent 40-year average

Example: LIBOR (London Interbank Offered Rates)—the wholesale cost of money in the London Interbank money market.
    Low – .186 July 2011
    High – 9.06 November 1989
    Median – 4.14

CYCLICAL vs. LIFE CYCLE MODELS

An economic cycle is a recurring macroeconomic event with high and low inflection points triggered by new, often different, macroeconomic or geopolitical events. It is a predictable model. In contrast, a life cycle is the inception, rise, peak, downfall and ultimate demise of a company or institution. Although not a recurring event, it is none the less also a predictable model.

Reversion to the mean does not apply to the "life cycle" model. Individual companies usually have a life cycle curve when the company—gradually in the case of manufacturing and rapidly in the case of high tech—builds market share and value until it reaches a peak or plateau. While Company A is reaching its peak, competitor Company B or even someone in their garage or college dorm room, has already found a better product that will result in the Company A's downfall and eventual demise until it is either acquired or goes out of business.

By knowing where a business—large or small—is in its life cycle, you can decide if you want to invest in it for the long term, the short term or avoid it all together.

Examples: Pan American Airlines, Polaroid, Kodak and Blockbuster Video, once great, "must own" stocks, have already reached the ends of their life cycles.

General Motors and Chrysler, whose stocks were once safe enough for "widows' and orphans' " portfolios, have only had a temporary stay of execution due to their taxpayer bailouts.

Microsoft and Apple have been climbing for a while, but still have some runway left until they get blindsided by the next great innovation emerging from a university dorm room.

Investing in any business without knowing where it is in its life cycle is like rolling the dice. Having said all this, I chose not to invest in the stock market.

> You build wealth by getting on and off the cycles before everyone else. It's like a roller coaster: when you hear the clicking stop... you get off. When you hear the screaming... it's too late. There should be no surprises for students of economic cycles.

ECONOMIC CYCLE WALL ART

Regardless of which economic cycle model you choose to use, the economic cycle diagram shown in Fig. 2-5 should be taped to the wall of your office or den with a sticky arrow indicating where you currently are situated on the economic cycle.

Only by having a map—and knowing where you are on the map—can you anticipate future events and be prepared to not only survive the cyclical changes, but to benefit from these changes.

Fig. 2-5   Economic Cycle

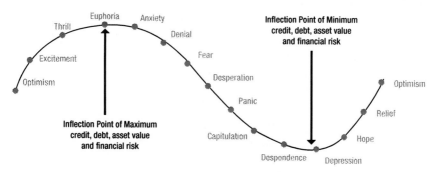

SUMMARY

Financial opportunities are always recurring and are always present somewhere. Economic cycles do exist.

Sun spot cycles were followed as far back as 325 BC. Economic cycles have been recorded since 1349 in Florence, Italy. Sir Isaac Newton lost his fortune when he failed to recognize the 1720 South Sea Company financial bubble.

But you don't need to be a genius to avoid getting caught up in an economic cycle; you just need to always be aware of where you are in relationship to the cycle.

There are over a dozen named popular economic cycle theories. The name of the cycle itself is not important. What is most important is to know exactly where you are on the current economic cycle at any given time.

Reliable indicators such as the Index of Leading Economic Indicators, the Yield Curve, the ISM and the VIX will help you locate your current position on the economic cycle. It is almost impossible to determine the actual inflection points (the top or bottom of the curves), but it is critical to have a clear understanding of which side of the curve you are on and which inflection point you are approaching.

Remember, since it is a cycle, you cannot apply linear concepts to nonlinear situations. Linear thought only leads people to believe that the good times will never stop and the bad times will never end. Likewise, you cannot apply static modeling to dynamic events, as seen when pundits speak of a "new metric," a "new paradigm" or a "new normal." Nothing should ever be a surprise to the student of economic cycles.

Just like understanding economic cycles will help you to anticipate near-term economic changes, understanding demographics will help you to both understand and anticipate the long-term trends.

The four words that have cost many investors their fortunes are:

"It's different this time."

The *two* words that have cost many investors their fortunes are:

"I do."

Building wealth begins with understanding assets and liabilities, economic cycles and demographics, making chapters 1, 2 and 3 all critical reading.

CHAPTER THREE

Understanding Demographics

In 2005, while I was performing my annual review of my books on demographics, Harry S. Dent's comment in his book *The Next Great Bubble Boom* (2004) jumped off the pages:

> "But here is the best strategy: don't expand your investment in properties in the latter years of this decade. In fact, sell off some of your properties by 2009 [written in 2004] to create excess cash and a very liquid balance sheet. Then you could have both cash and borrowing power during the early stages of the downturn to buy rental properties or properties that could be converted to rental properties at greatly depreciated costs and offer very low-rent apartments to boomers and other people struggling in the downturn…. If you were looking to sell your business, 2008 or 2009 would likely be the best time." [1]

I made a careful assessment of where I was on my wall-mounted economic cycle curve (the roller coaster's clicking had stopped) and reviewed the demographic data so clearly presented by Dent Research. I adopted my new motto: "Get out before '08… or it's too late."

Over a period of 16 months, just prior to the 2008 economic down turn, I sold over $20 million of my commercial real estate. I spent the next four years riding out the Great Recession pool side at the Ritz Carlton Hotel in Sarasota, FL. Near the end of the recession I (sadly) sold my luxury hotel condo and moved into an apartment.

In anticipation of the economic recovery, I put my money back to work in industrial property and spent the Ritz-Carlton money installing railroad track to my seaport-based warehouses (my office referred to it as "The Ritz Railroad"). I plan to move back to the Ritz Carlton later on in this cycle when the buying and investing opportunities once again become slim and the "stupid money" arrives on the scene.

It's not rocket science.

It's not easy... but it *is* simple.

It's about asset investing, economic cycles and demographics. You can do it, too.

AGE AND CONSUMER EARNING

Harry S. Dent has brought clarity to the social science of demographics. Dent Research uses the U.S. Government Consumer

Fig. 3-1 Top 10% of Households, Income by Age

■ Share of household 10-year cohort earning $100,000 and over

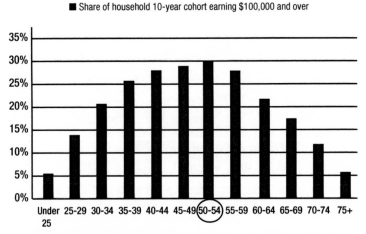

Data Source: U.S. Census Bureau, 2012, Dent Research

Expenditure Survey data dating back to 1984 to illustrate how one's age correlates with expected earnings (Fig. 3-1).

AGE AND CONSUMER SPENDING

Dent also uses demographic data to show how the stage of life determines spending patterns. This "Consumer Life Cycle" is shown in Fig. 3-2. As people move through predictable stages of life, which correspond with different ages, spending habits also change in very predictable ways. How we spend our money at each stage is both predictable and consistent, and this data can be used to forecast economic and social changes in the decades to come.

Fig. 3-2 Consumer Life Cycle

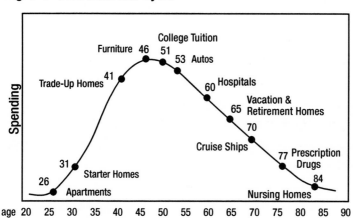

Data Source: U.S. Census Bureau, Dent Research

Dent has shown that the first acceleration in an individual's spending comes when they enter the workforce around age 20. With marriage, at the average age of 26, their spending significantly accelerates with apartment rentals and purchases of automobiles, furnishings and durable goods.

In their late 20s, they have children and their spending again increases and becomes more domestic and family-oriented.

At age 34, on average, they buy their first homes and assume debt at a faster rate. This period is the time of their fastest debt accumulation. More recently, the accumulation of student debt in their early 20s has become a factor. Around age 45 they purchase their largest house and buy higher-end furnishings. Dent reports that spending peaks at ages 47 to 52, or age 48 on average.

As Dent's "Spending Wave" (discussed in the next section) of 47- to 52-year-old high earners and spenders ages, their impact on the economy is predictable. At age 55 they reach their peak rate of investing, at age 59 their peak power in business and politics, and by age 60, half will retire from their main careers. Since 2008, this retirement age has been increasing and can be expected to continue to do so for years to come as the resources of retirement become less reliable and, in some cases, diminished or maybe even extinguished.

CONSUMER SPENDING WAVE

Harry S. Dent, Jr. is the founder of Dent Research, an economic research firm specializing in demographic trends and their application to predicting business cycles and long-term economic trends.

Starting in his book *The Great Boom Ahead*, Dent diagrammed the generational "Spending Wave" (supercharged by the Baby Boomer generation), which he based on demographic data. The Spending Wave accounted for the spending effect on various sectors of the economy—both in the past and into the future. It allows for documentation of people's predictable spending habits throughout their lives. As such, it seems to be our simplest and most powerful, long range forecasting tool.

Looking back on Fig. 3-2, Dent's Consumer Life Cycle illustrates the Spending Wave best. When you use the Spending Wave chart as a reference and superimpose either the average age of the Boomer generation or the average age of the Millennial generation, you can fully understand consumer spending in the past, present and into the future.

Demographic studies show that age determines spending and group spending determines the direction of the economy. In his book *Wealth Shift*, Christopher D. Brooke (2006) states: "Remember, this isn't anecdotal. This is demographics. Millions and millions of people all doing about the same thing and spending in about the same ways. Now collect a sizable percentage of these millions around certain areas, and what happened was entirely predictable. The same can be said for what the boomers are moving toward: it is predictable." [2]

As you follow the peak of the Baby Boomer generation from the 1950s to 2014, you can understand how they caused the spikes in purchases of baby food in the 1950s, records and jeans in the 1960s, minivans in the 1980s, motorcycles in the 1990s (peak age for buying motorcycles is age 48) and hearing aids in 2013. In the field of healthcare alone, we can see how the Baby Boomer bulge, as it travelled along the age timeline, caused consecutive innovations such as pediatric care, fertility research and procedures, liposuction and face lifts—and finally, hearing aids and erectile dysfunction medication.

To state it even more simply, (although less elegantly) the Boomer generation drove the diaper market in the early 1950s when they were in their "terrible 3s" and they will again fuel the diaper market in the early 2040s when they are in their "naughty 90s."

In *Wealth Shift*, author Christopher Brooke sums it up:

> "Here's the bottom line: age determines the spending, and spending en masse determines the direction of the economy. The good news for forward looking investors is that age is about as certain as… well, death and taxes." [3]

PREDICTIONS BASED ON DEMOGRAPHICS

In his 1993 book *The Great Boom Ahead*, Dent correctly predicted the "Roaring 90s" lasting up to year 2000. Using his demographic Spending Wave tool, Dent describes an economy up to 46 years into the future. His statements, made in 1993, seem eerie in 2014: "However, the bust that follows the boom will be every bit as devastating as the opportunity will be salutary—starting around 2008, [remember this was written in 1993] when the height of the baby boom passes through its spending peak. That's when I predict the onset of the next Great Depression." [4]

"So you can expect a major economic downturn starting around 2008 and lasting to around 2022–2023. No amount of government stimulus will prevent it [again written in 1993; our current Federal Reserve Board must not have read this], just as it didn't prevent the Great Depression of the 1930s." [5]

Later, in 1998 he wrote *The Roaring 2000s*, and continued applying his demographic data to economic forecasts: "Somewhere around late 2006 to late 2008… it will be time to begin making major shifts in your long-term portfolio and asset allocation. You should be increasingly cautious and conservative as our economy enters a deflationary period of decline." [6]

In his most recent book, *The Demographic Cliff* (2014), Dent forecasts several years of deflation resulting from the debt deleveraging and diminished spending of the Baby Boomer generation, who are retiring at a rate of 7,000 a day. He calls for another economic boom in the 2030s, corresponding with the Millennial Generation Spending Wave as they go through their peak spending years of ages 48 through 52.

Demographics and Real Estate

The Baby Boomer generation is getting older. They no longer need or want to care for oversized homes and they are downsizing. There will be a near-term (2014–2018) demand for these trophy houses as the most successful Boomers sell their businesses, cash in their stocks, and pony up for one more spending spree. After 2018, the older and early retiring Baby Boomer generation will be able to unload their dinosaur houses onto the younger Boomers retiring behind them, but that window of opportunity will quickly close.

Whenever you make a large purchase, whether it is going into your Asset Box (rental property) or into your Liability Box (an expensive toy), you should always ask yourself the following question: "Who will buy this when the time comes for me to sell it?"

The Millennial Generation is too smart to buy large, high-cost, high-maintenance homes—even if they could afford them. Between the education loans and the debt they are inheriting from the Baby Boomer generation, these extravagant luxuries will always be out of their reach. Besides, the Millennial Generation is not willing to put in the time, effort and selfless sacrifice to acquire and maintain either trophy homes or expensive toys. They are not willing to compromise their sensible and pragmatic way of life where experiences and relationships trump material possessions.

The Millennial Generation will be buying low-maintenance, energy-efficient homes that will allow them to spend more of their spare time and money on more interesting experiences in life. The tail end of the Boomer generation will find it challenging to unload their big "McMansions," lumbering motor coaches and "Dock Queen" yachts onto a generation shopping for small, low-maintenance homes and energy-efficient vehicles with roof racks for their kayaks.

THE DEMOGRAPHIC INVESTMENT VACUUM

Harry S. Dent's recent book *The Demographic Cliff* (2014) and Warren Brussee's book *The Second Great Depression* (2005) both describe the stock market as being a Baby Boomer's game. This generation will soon be moving out of equities and into income stream investments such as laddered bonds and annuities (ugh!). People invest in the stock market during their high income years, ages 35–55, and that demographic wave will soon be marching on. As the Boomers age out and start heading for the exits, there will be no one from the Millennial Generation waiting in line to take their place.

The Millennials watched the Boomers suffer losses of up to 40 percent in both 2000 and again in 2008. It is a generation saddled with high education loans and poor near-term employment prospects. Investing is on their to-do list, far below their goals of moving out of their parents' home and buying a reliable car. In their short life-times, they have witnessed huge stock market losses and they have yet to live through a sustained stock market upturn. They have been exposed to a barrage of stories on the Internet involving insider trad-ing, corporate malfeasance, and large corporate bailouts—none of which make a case for them to turn over their hard-earned money to the Wall Street Boys.

All the demographic data points to there being a big sucking sound when the Boomers leave Wall Street.

Personally, I will be investing in well-located "workforce" (not low income or subsidized) site-built housing in com-munities with the promise of job growth. I will also invest in small, inexpensive, low-maintenance homes in warm climates with ample future water supply and within a bus ride or walking distance of a Wal-mart, Walgreens, CVS and casual dining restaurants. I will also invest in land lease and communities (midrange mobile home parks) where I will own the land and rent the lots but will not have to deal with the issues of maintaining the structures, the HVAC or appliances. As I get older, I will invest less directly into assets and more into providing the debt (mortgage financing) for this safe asset class to even further distance myself from the day-to-day operational responsibilities, while still having my money safely positioned in what I consider to be the asset classes of the future.

MIGRATION TRENDS

The migration trend, for both businesses and the retiring Baby Boomer generation, is toward the Sun Belt, especially the south eastern

U.S. These trends are supported by Christopher Brooke in his book *Wealth Shift* (2006): "The current housing trends in warm weather areas like Florida, Phoenix, the Gulf Coast, the southeastern United States and Las Vegas offer investors a no-brainer lesson in the time and a lifestyle: folks dislike the cold weather." [7]

THE DEMOGRAPHIC GROUPS

The specific characteristics of the generational groups were best described by Tim Elmore in his 2010 book *Generation iY*. The characteristics of each generation are listed below. [8]

The "Greatest" or "G I" Generation
Born: 1909–1924

They saw their future as uncertain and shunned excessive debt.

This generation, which spent its adolescence in the Great Depression and its youth during World War II, will go on to be the only generation to enjoy retirement funded almost entirely by the following generation. They deserved it.

The "Silent" Generation
Born: 1925–1945

They can be described as being much like their previous generation with the same values.

"Baby Boomer" or "Boomer" Generation
Born: 1946–1964

View of work: "I live to work."

They purchased on credit and accumulated debt. The feelings of entitlement for pensions and elderly healthcare would surely bankrupt America, but the larger Millennial generation's attendance at the voting booths will put the brakes on the entitlement spending which the country will not be able to afford.

The "Generation X"
Born: 1965–1983

View of work: "I work to live."

Having larger and more financially influential generations both before and after them has caused Generation X to be marginalized by both demographers and consumer product merchandisers.

The "Millennial" or "Y" Generation
Born: 1983–2002

View of work: "I work to make a difference."

Millennials can be described as being team players, globally connected, on 24/7, and interested in the greater good. They prefer work parameters, work schedules that fit their lifestyles and they covet positive reinforcement and praise. Access is more important to them than ownership. They value experiences over trophy assets. They strive for a work/life balance.

In *Generation iY*, Elmore puts it into perspective best by listing the following characteristics of the "Millennial" generation: [9]

They never rode a bike without a helmet.
They never rode in a car without a seatbelt.
They have never known a world
without the Internet.

George Foreman has always been
a barbeque salesman.

In the United Kingdom, Millennials who still live at home as adults are called "KIPPERS," short for "Kids In Parents' Pockets Eroding Retirement Savings." They were often raised by "helicopter" (as in hovering) parents and they had every minute of their day structured, often involving a team activity.

In their book *Millennials Rising: The Next Great Generation* (2000), authors Neil Howe and William Strauss note that by 2025, Millennials will dominate the teaching profession, school boards and juries. They will comprise almost 20 percent of our national leaders.

Howe and Strauss stated: "A new middle class will emerge. With thirtyish Millennials filling the lesser paid ranks, a distinctly modern form of unionism could resurrect class consciousness, culminating in political class warfare and demands for higher taxes on rich generation X tycoons and reduced benefits for affluent old Boomers, whose old-age entitlements might be resented by generation X'ers and the Millennials alike. With the disappearance of the generations to whom the original Social Security and Medicare 'promises' were made, Millennials may feel free to press for a 'new deal' that would reduce payouts to Boomers and generation X'ers in return for better long-term treatment of Millennials, who, by then will embody America's hopes for its national future." [10]

DEMOGRAPHICS AND ECONOMIC FORECASTING

Generations of varying sizes will age and have predictable cycles of spending based on their needs and wants. The stock market pundits, TV talking heads and most economic forecasters are always predicting the short term—the next two or three quarters ahead.

The long-term forecast can be more reliably made because of its dependency on the basics of demographics and economic cycles, and not on the moods and self-interests of the high-velocity Wall Street traders.

It's been proven that the spending fluctuations of the long-term economy have been influenced by the number of those aged 45 to

54, the big spenders in the population at the time. This demographic data can be applied—along with the understanding of economic cycles—to forecast the economy years into the future. The major, unknown wildcard will always be the geopolitical events that can throw a wrench into even the best forecast.

The generation that shaped America through its sheer size and synchronous spending is about to clock out... retire. In *Wealth Shift* (2006) Brooke writes: "Their predictable, age-based spending is driving the economy. The looming question is what's going to happen when they stop working and start spending like retired people. They will save differently. They will invest differently." [11]

"The first Baby Boomers turn 62 in 2008, and the retirement parade begins. Every single day of that year and for years to follow, between 8,000 and 10,000 Baby Boomers will clock out. Every day, another 8,000 to 10,000 people take their earned incomes away from the Treasury's reach." [12]

"Every day, between $432 million and $540 million in personal income will drop from the economy and evaporate as a source of revenue to the Treasury. That's every day." [13]

"The bottom line is that we're going to have a lot of high-tax rate earners leaving the system and being replaced by 10 to 20 percent fewer, earning half as much, taxed at half the rate. The country's net taxable income is going to simply plummet." [14]

In *The Great Bust Ahead* (2002) Daniel A. Arnold also writes: "That these big-spending Americans control the long-term peaks and valleys of the economy (the booms and busts), is now clearly beyond dispute. It really is as straightforward as that." [15]

Arnold goes on to conclude: "It's not the Baby Boomers retiring that is going to collapse the economy... it's the catastrophic decline in the number of big-spending, GDP-driving 45 to 54-year-old Boomers that is the problem." [16]

ENTITLEMENTS

In their book *The Fourth Turning* (1997), authors Strauss and Howe state: "The economy will not keep growing as smoothly as the actuaries now assume—and critical events will force the government to reshuffle all its spending priorities. At that point, no one will be entitled to anything: those in need will only be 'authorized' something." [17]

Elderly Boomers will collide with underfunded federal pensions, private pension and healthcare systems in 2016.

By 2020, younger workers will need to hand over between 30 and 40 percent of their payroll to provide the Boomers with their promised entitlements.

Boomers will not have enough control at the voting booth to make it politically possible to impose such a tax burden on the dual income, Millennial generation household. The affluent Boomers will receive little economic recompense for a lifetime of payroll taxes paid to support the prior generation.

Tax laws are not biblical laws: they can be changed in response to changing conditions and changes in voter's sentiments. In the *Wall Street Journal*'s editorial "The Entitlement Panic" (*WSJ* August 22, 2006), the authors state that entitlement benefits are not a contractual government obligation in the same sense as a treasury bond. In its landmark 1960 decision, *Flemming v. Nestor*, the U.S. Supreme Court ruled that there is no such legal right to Social Security. It is precisely the unsustainability of these future benefits that will make reform unattractive, as younger people realize they have no hope of ever getting what they are currently paying for.

And so, the elderly, white-hair Baby Boomers will take to the streets, much like they did in the late 1960s, but this time with their walkers, hurling empty Metamucil cans and trying to smash store and bank windows with their canes.

PREDICTIONS FOR THE YEAR 2020

There is a conspicuous absence of demographic data describing the time period of 2018–2022. Most of the demographic information in print sees this as a time of at least financial challenge, if not significant geopolitical turmoil.

In his book *The Next Great Bubble Boom* (2004), Harry S. Dent describes a "second great crash 2020–2022," replete with a stock market and disinflation forces unresponsive to government stimulation. He, along with other authors, brings forth the geopolitical wildcard:

> "This will represent a time period when the greatest threats from the Middle East in large-scale terrorism and the Far East military (North Korea and/or China) could come to the U.S. and Europe. The seeds of World War III, if it is to occur, are most likely to emerge here." [18]

> This same theme is addressed in the 500-page classic *Generations* (1991), where authors Strauss and Howe use a demographic "Millennial Cycle" to predict that "the early 2020s appear fateful.... The crisis of 2020 will be a major turning point in American history and an adrenaline-filled moment of trial." [19]

PREDICTIONS FOR BEYOND 2023

Most demographic data indicates long-term economic prosperity for the United States beginning after resolution of the economic/geopolitical issues of the early 2020s and lasting well into the 2030s. A key demographic difference between the U.S. and Europe is that the U.S. has a much higher rate of immigration of educated and talented people from all over the world. Immigrants into Europe are generally uneducated and are seeking refuge from a problem, whereas immigrants to the U.S. are generally better educated and are seeking opportunity.

SUMMARY

Demography is destiny. It is the looking glass into our future. It is the statistical data of a population.

The stage of one's life determines one's spending habits. As a large group of individuals travel through successive age levels, both their spending and its effect on the economy are predictable.

Business and individual migration is toward the south eastern U.S.

The past five major generational groups have interesting, specific characteristics.

The tail end of the Baby Boomer generation will find it challenging to unload their big "McMansions," lumbering motor coaches and "Dock Queen" yachts onto the Millennials. The Millennials will have much less money and they will be shopping for small, low-maintenance homes and energy-efficient vehicles that include roof racks for their kayaks.

The generation that has shaped America is clocking out... retiring at a rate of over 7,000 per day. A large group of high-tax-paying earners are leaving the income tax system and are being replaced by those taxed at half the rate; while at the same time, the spending wave of high-earning, high-spending Boomers between the ages of 45 and 54 is rapidly diminishing.

The combination of the Baby Boomers' dramatically increasing, under-funded retirement, along with their medical entitlement needs and wants, will surely result in a fiscal "Perfect Storm" that will only be resolved by the Millennials at the voting booth.

Wall Street's "retail" (street code for "clueless") investors have always been the Baby Boomer generation. As the Boomers pull their money out of their 401(k)s and IRAs to cover their retirement living, they will be selling into a vacuum. The Millennials saw what happened to their parents in 1987, 2000 and 2008 and they are way too smart to play that game.

It is likely there will be economic and geopolitical strife around 2018–2022. If you are invested in income-producing, hard assets you will be one of the fortunate, few, sideline spectators.

By understanding both the forward-marching forces of demographics and the predictability of the economic cycles, you will be able to mentally superimpose these two tools and bring the vagaries of forecasting into focus. You will want to make a concerted effort to review the demographic books once a year and check the financial cycle tools (yield curve, ISM, VIX) once a month—much like one checks a compass or GPS—to help you keep your financial bearings.

Remember:

- Put your money into assets.
- Know where you are on the economic cycle.
- Demography is destiny.

Building wealth is all about understanding assets and liabilities, economic cycles and demographics. Your understanding of chapters 1, 2 and 3 is critical to building your wealth.

PART II
KEEP YOUR WEALTH

CHAPTER FOUR

Redistribution and *Your* Wealth

The first three chapters have illustrated how to build wealth by putting your money into assets instead of liabilities, being aware of the implications of the coming demographic changes and always knowing where you are on the economic cycle.

The ultimate goal is to enjoy spending all of your hard-earned money, and this concept is discussed in the last chapter.

But between earning it and enjoying spending it, there are very real risks of having it taken away from you and redistributed to others. This chapter will show you both the ongoing and planned programs the government has for redistributing your earned money to someone else before *you* get a chance to... *spend it all.*

In his book *The Constitution of Liberty* (1960, 2012), Friedrich A. Hayek states: "Liberty not only means that the individual has both the opportunity and the burden of choice; it also means that he must bear the consequences of his actions and will receive praise or blame for them. Liberty and responsibility are inseparable. A free society will not function or maintain itself unless its members regard it as a right that each individual occupy the position that results from his action and accept it as due to his own action." [1]

ROBBING PETER TO PAY PAUL—AND YOU'RE PETER

If, financially, you are in the lower 60 percent of retirees and have less than $12,000 saved for retirement, there's good news: you have nothing to worry about. Somebody else will be financing your 20-plus years of retirement.

If you are in the upper 15 percent of those retiring and have over $300,000 saved for retirement, there's bad news: *you* are that somebody else who will be financing those 20-plus years of someone else's retirement. It is because they need it; you have "more than enough" and the government is planning to redistribute it because it is the most "fair" and "equitable" solution to an almost unsolvable problem for the federal government.

They're going to rob Peter to pay Paul… and you're Peter. It is called redistribution. Don't get mad, get ready. Get ready to enjoy your hard-earned money and spend it all.

INEQUALITY OF ECONOMIC OUTCOME

Today, just months before the U.S. mid-term elections, the term "inequality" has become the political hot button for those to push when looking to garner class warfare votes to keep their Washington, D.C. jobs. Since I'm not running for election, I can drill down to the actual, although politically incorrect, reasons for economic "inequality," such as inequality of education, inequality of skill, inequality of work effort and inequality of time spent actually *working*. Hang on… this chapter might be a rough ride for some of you.

In 1848, Karl Marx—19th century social scientist, historian and socialist thinker—wrote in his *Communist Manifesto*:

> "From each according to his ability, to each according to his need." [2]

Nineteenth century French political thinker and author of *Democracy in America* (1835), Alexis De Tocqueville was an early witness to America's fixation on equality of outcome, rather than equality of opportunity. He is often quoted as having said:

> "Americans are so enamored with equality that they would rather be equal in slavery than unequal in freedom." [3]

Economics Nobel Prize laureate Milton Friedman stated in *Free to Choose* (1980):

> "A society that puts equality—in the sense of equality of outcome—ahead of freedom will end up with neither equality nor freedom." [4]

Matt Walsh, editor and publisher of the *Business Observer* (FL) stated in his November 15, 2013 editorial, "How Did This Happen? A Cosmic Collision":

> "The world is a bell curve; our nation is a bell curve. Americans are a bell curve."

> "From the beginning of the biblical times to today, there have always been poor people, middle class people and rich people. There have always been really sick or handicapped people, healthy people and super healthy people. There have always been below average intelligence people, average intelligence people and really smart people. There have always been lazy people, average achievers and extraordinary achievers. And always will be." [5]

Statists in the government think they can reduce bell curves to flat lines so that everyone is equal.

INCOME INEQUALITY DUE TO EDUCATION

There is also a close correlation between household income and the unequal level of education. The U.S. Census Bureau Statistical

Abstract of the United States: 2012 (2009 data) reports the median household income for those without a high school education to be $21,635 compared with a median household income of $123,784 for those with a professional degree.

INEQUALITY OF WORK EFFORT

In his 1/8/2014 *Wall Street Journal* opinion piece titled "How The War on Poverty Was Lost," Heritage Foundation senior research fellow Robert Rector uses U.S. Census data to show that even when not in a recession, an adult in the average poor family works just 800 hours a year, or 16 hours a week, inevitably leading to decreasing earnings and increasing dependency.

Economists Mark Aguiar and Erik Hurst reviewed time-use surveys taken from 1965 through 2005. In their article *Measuring Trends in Leisure: The Allocation of Time Over Five Decades,* they report finding that between 1985 and 2005, men who had not completed high school increased their leisure time by eight hours per week, while men who had completed college decreased their leisure time by six hours per week. [6]

Recent data presented by the Manhattan Institute Senior Fellow Diana Furchtgott-Roth (*Wall Street Journal,* December 15, 2013) revealed the following about minimum wages:

The top 20 percent of households have on average:

▸ 3.1 persons/household
▸ 2 income earners/household
▸ 11 percent own a house without a mortgage

The bottom 20 percent of households have an average of:

▸ 1.7 persons per household
▸ 0.5 income earners per household
▸ 28 percent own their home without a mortgage

The bottom 20 percent has a low reported household income because it is made up of fewer people (such as students working part time) and fewer income earners (such as retired couples or individuals).

Numerous studies have confirmed that both the top 20 percent and the bottom 20 percent of households, ranked by household income, are transient: up to 80 percent of those earning less tend to move up the economic ladder and those near the top are often there for only one year as a result of a once-in-a-lifetime sale of a small business or family property.

The top 20 percent has higher reported household income for obvious reasons: they have two full time (and up to four full time and part time combined) income earners per household compared with 0.5 earners per household in the lowest 20 percent group.

Yes, there is inequality of both income and wealth in America, and it is highly correlated with the amount of time and effort those in the household are willing or able to spend working.

The U.S. Census Bureau data, although factual, should not be used to indict or pass judgment on those in the lower income households who are categorized as "not working." Some may have good reasons for not working, such as being full-time students, those with legitimate physical or psychiatric disabilities or those of advanced age and generalized, chronic poor health.

> Personally, I have never accomplished any of the goals in my life, the reason being that each time I approached my goal, I chose to move the goalposts further away. Financial success involves never actually reaching your goal.

INEQUALITY OF SPENDING

The high earners in the top 20 percent group also spend differently. The top 5 percent account for 40 percent of consumer spending, while the bottom 80 percent of earners account for only 40 percent of consumer spending.

INEQUALITY OF CHARITABLE GIVING

Regarding charitable donations, the lower-middle class gives a greater percent of their net worth and income than do the wealthy. But charitable bequests (the money people give away *after* they die only because they can't take it with them) are more concentrated, with the wealthiest 1.4 percent of decedents accounting for about 86 percent of all charitable bequests.

INEQUALITY OF TAX PAYMENTS

Economists say that income tax in an economy is always a zero sum game; that is, the balance sheet always equals zero. The government cannot give money to someone without first taking it away from someone else who earned it in the first place.

In *Capitalism 4.0* (2010) economist Anatole Kaletsky makes note of the federal income tax distribution:

> ▸ Top 1 percent pays 40 percent of tax revenue
> ▸ Top 5 percent pays 60 percent of tax revenue
> ▸ Top 25 percent pays 97 percent of tax revenue

In 2010, the top 10 percent of taxpayers accounted for 71 percent of all income tax revenue to the government, up from 55 percent in 1986.

A *Wall Street Journal* editorial "Their Fair Share" (July 21, 2008) stated:

> "The top 1 percent earned 22 percent of all reported income. But they also paid a share of the taxes not far from double their share of the income. There is a rapid turnover in the ranks of the highest income earners... People who started in 1 percent of income in the 1980s and 90s suffered the largest declines and earnings of any group... It's hard to stay King of the Hill in America for long." [7]

This transient characteristic also applies to the bottom 20 percent of wage earners. This is a group that has a large component of newly poor and temporarily poor (students, temporarily unemployed, temporarily disabled) in addition to the multi-generational, habitually poor in the group.

A *Wall Street Journal* editorial "How Much the Rich Pay" (January 20, 2012) reported:

> "The Congressional Budget Office (CBO) recently examined the distribution of federal taxes on various income groups.... And the rich pay more, which is probably why the press didn't report it.... The poorest 20 percent on average paid a net negative income tax rate of 5.6 percent because of the checks they received for tax credits that are 'refundable.' These are essentially transfer payments redistributing income from the rich and middle class to the poor.... As for all federal taxes, CBO found that in 2007 the top 1 percent paid an average rate of a little less than 30 percent, compared with 15.1 percent from middle income earners.... CBO takes account of payroll taxes, which moves the rate of the lowest 20 percent of earners into positive territory at 4.5 percent... Average effective tax rate on the richest 1 percent is already twice as high as that of the middle class." [8]

LABOR FORCE NONPARTICIPATION

American industriousness fascinated the rest of the world, and it seemed that no other American quality was seen so consistently as being exceptional.

The U.S. was once viewed as the home of the "employment miracle." Europeans have long been disdainful of the American work ethic and have often smugly stated "Europeans work to live. Americans live to work."

As recently as 1989, the U.S. was a leader in workforce participation and employment rates among the world's most developed countries. That is no longer the case. As of 2014 men have been withdrawing from the workforce for five decades—in good times and bad, in tight and slack labor markets, in periods of Keynesian stimulation and austerity. The labor participation rate is the lowest it has been since 1978. Demographic changes can accommodate for some of this decrease in labor force participation (i.e., the Baby Boomer generation retiring), but that does not account for the persistent decrease in workforce participation by the 23- to 43-year-old age group. Average participation rates in 16 comparison countries are 4 to 6 points higher than they are in the U.S. Last year the U.S. ranked in the bottom third for percentage of women and last for percentage of men participating in the U.S. workforce.

Jonathan R. Laing authored an article in *Barron's* (October 28, 2013) titled "Slowing to a Crawl." In his article he wrote:

> "The labor-participation rate of Americans (the Bureau of Labor Statistics computes the number by dividing all workers by the number of Americans over 16 years of age) has been falling steadily for the past seven years from 66.2% in 2006 to 63.2% in August of this year [2013]."

> "This can't all be attributed to layoffs during the Great Recession of 2007–2009 since we are well into a recovery. Nor have baby boomers' retirements begun to hit with ferocity yet. The leading edge of that generation only reached retirement age in 2011."

> "JPMorgan's report notes that the falling participation rate has hit prime-aged 25-to-54-year-old workers as hard over the past year as the overall labor force. Their participation rate dropped from 83% in the fourth quarter of 2006 to 81% in the third quarter of 2013." [9]

A 2013 Cato Institute report found that a family of three receiving the maximum government assistance could receive $63,000 in benefits, while an employed worker with a family of three had an average income of $57,000. With today's 126 government programs that disincentivize work, the head of a household of three would think twice before taking a job with a 40-hour work week that pays less than $63,000.

More people are being incentivized to stop pulling the wagon and instead are climbing aboard and joining those riding in the wagon, as we discuss later in this chapter.

THE VOLUNTARILY "DISABLED"

In his book *The Great Degeneration* (2012), Harvard University History professor Niall Ferguson notes that the U.S. economy created 2.4 million jobs from June 2009 to June 2012, while 3.3 million Americans enrolled in disability benefit programs.

More generous unemployment benefits tend to increase unemployment counts since workers must be looking for work to qualify for unemployment benefits. With disability insurance, the opposite applies: to qualify applicants must demonstrate they cannot work, and they cannot be looking for work.

IT'S CALLED WORK

President Reagan famously quipped: "A good job is the best social program."

The late economist Robert Theobald in *The Rapids of Change* (1987) defines work:

> "Work is defined as something that people do not want to do and money is the reward that compensates for the unpleasantness of work." [10]

> In *How to Get Rich and Stay Rich* (1996) Fred J. Young states: "Most of the great fortunes I know about were started by someone who worked long hours, scrimped and

saved, and made unbelievable sacrifice to get the fortune started." [11]

TRANSFER (WELFARE) PROGRAMS

The Cato Institute counts 126 separate federal antipoverty programs, including 72 that provide "cash or in-kind benefits to individuals."

Looking at average benefits received and taxes paid per person and per tax dollar paid is revealing. In *"A Nation of Takers,"* Eberstadt reported the following 2004 figures:

Taxes paid and benefits received per person:		
Top 20 percent of earners	$21,721 taxes paid	$6,704 benefits received
Middle 20 percent of earners	$6,316 taxes paid	$7,905 benefits received
Bottom 20 percent of earners	$2,399 taxes paid	$16,345 benefits received
Benefits received per one dollar of tax paid:		
Top 20 percent of tax payers	$.31	
Middle 20 percent of tax payers	$1.25	
Bottom 20 percent of tax payers	$6.82	

This huge transfer of money and benefits is not included in the household income figures used to argue the case of income inequality. This was based on 2004 data; the figures are skewed much more now in 2014 due to the explosion in the issuance of EBT cards (food stamps), not to mention expansion of the other 125 government transfer (welfare) programs.

SOCIAL SECURITY: INTERGENERATIONAL DEBT TRANSFER

In 1906 Dr. William Osler was one of the first to promote retirement from work at the age of 60 to make more jobs available to those who were younger and unemployed.

The first Social Security premiums were collected in 1937 and the first benefit check was written in 1942. The first Social Security beneficiary was Ida M. Fuller (1874–1975). As a Vermont legal secretary she paid $24.75 in Social Security taxes over three years and lived to be 100 years old, having collected over $20,000 in benefits payout alone. It was a Ponzi scheme right from the start.

The Social Security program was described as "social insurance" and it was originally sold to the American public as if it were an insurance program. Social Security withholding taxes were "premiums" and payments were "benefits." In reality, it was a transfer program much like writing a check to your elderly parents with an additional handling fee to Washington, DC.

Social Security was declared to be unconstitutional by the First Circuit Court of Appeals in 1937, but the decision was later reversed (*Doris v Boston & Maine R Co* and *Doris v Edison Electric Illuminating Co. of Boston et al*).

THE SOCIAL SECURITY NEST EGG MYTH

First you need to dispense with the Social Security myth you have been told for the last 40 years. There is no "lockbox" into which the money deducted from your paycheck has been going. There is no Social Security bank account or retirement account with your name and Social Security number on it. You have been lied to by your elected officials. You need to just get over it and move on.

Social Security was simply a tax on working folks used as a slush fund for the federal government with some of it actually going to support your parents or grandparents. It worked well, probably for one generation:

those who retired between 1960 and 1998. Those retiring after 2015 will live to see how all Ponzi schemes end, and it is never pretty.

Social Security was never meant to be a retirement program; it was supposed to be a safety net for orphans, widows and the truly disabled. Over the years, politicians gained popularity and kept their jobs by expanding this program to cover an ever-increasing number of voters. Those who are dependent on Social Security are compelled to vote for those who promise not to stop or decrease that entitlement.

In the near future there will be no choice but to "means test" both Social Security and Medicare. The days of a Warren Buffett or other wealthy retiree cruising around in their gated community in golf carts having their retirement lifestyle and medical care subsidized by the struggling, dual-income Millennial generation will screech to a halt. In 2020, the 77 million (and decreasing daily) Baby Boomer voters will be outnumbered at the voting booth by the 85 million (and increasing) Millennials. The campaigning politicians will no longer be incentivized to protect those precious "entitlements."

The old, gray-haired, tired, white male faces in Congress will be replaced with young, multiracial, bright and eager faces that will be pragmatic and will pull the country from the brink of fiscal ruin. They will have no choice but to throw the Baby Boomers under the bus. Social Security is a Ponzi scheme and the Boomer generation is too late to the game.

While today's 65-year-olds will receive an average net lifetime benefit of $327,400, the children born today will experience lifetime net losses of $420,600 as they struggle to pay the bills of the aging Americans.

And how does this square with the Millennial generation? Will they vote to fund and support this with their own hard-earned income? The income of the young couple going to work each morning is being taxed at a rate of up to 38 percent while the retired Baby Boomers living off dividends and passive income are being taxed at the 20-percent capital gains rate or 0-percent federal taxes from Treasury bond yields.

With intergenerational debt transfer such as Social Security, the high public debt allows the current generation to live their lifestyle at the expense of those too young to vote. But eventually they *will* grow up, and they *will* vote to suit their own financial self-interest and the voting Millennial Generation will outnumber the voting Baby Boomers beginning in 2020.

In *The Great Degeneration* (2012), Niall Ferguson reports that when the unfunded liabilities of Social Security, Medicare and Medicaid are added to the $17 trillion current public debt, the sum is a staggering $200 trillion, or 13 times the public debt as reported by the U.S. Treasury Department. This does not include the $38 trillion of state and local government unfunded liabilities.

In a September 8, 2013 *Wall Street Journal* op-ed entitled "How to Maximize Your Social Security Benefits," author Anne Tergesen reviewed five online Social Security programs for couples and projected a lifetime cumulative Social Security benefit for a couple ranging from between $763,000 and $773,000. That is only the Social Security benefits. Add in the couple's Medicare benefits and you get the "Million-Dollar Couple."

THE ALLEGED POOR

In *Economic Facts and Fallacies* (2007), Thomas Sowell notes:

> "Since the people in the bottom 20 percent of income received more than two thirds of their income from transfer payments, leaving those cash payments out of the statistics clearly exaggerates their poverty—and leaving out in-kind transfers as well, such as subsidized housing, distorts their situation even more." [12]

It is not widely known, or at least understood, that the U.S. Census Bureau uses a definition of "money income" that excludes taxes, which skews the income figures for high earners. It also excludes transfer payments like Medicaid, Medicare, nutrition assistance, the Earned

Income Tax Credit and employer-provided benefits such as health insurance, that skew down the perceived plight of the alleged poor.

In his *Wall Street Journal* opinion article "Hurdles For The New Line on Poverty" (September 21, 2013), Carl Bailik also takes note of the fact that the "Poverty Line" devised by the Social Security Administration in 1963 fails to account for the many non-cash government-subsidized benefits such as food stamps, housing and of course medical care provided to the poor with taxpayer dollars.

The Census Bureau now reports the poverty rate, and since 2011 it has set the poverty line at the level of expenditures on essential items at the thirty-third percentile, meaning two thirds of households spend more on these goods. (Only a government statistician could dream up this one.) The new government measure labels even more citizens—16 percent—as being below the new and higher poverty line.

In 2008, New York City created its own—and not surprisingly higher—poverty line which designates 23 percent of its citizens as being poor, compared with 18 percent when the federal guidelines are used.

A more concrete picture of America's "poor" is revealed by using the Census data reported to the Dallas Federal Reserve (2005).

Of those living below the federal poverty line in 2005:

    99 percent have a refrigerator

    99 percent have a stove

    96 percent have a landline telephone

    82 percent have climate control

    78 percent have a DVD player (today's MP3 player)

    73 percent have a microwave oven

    57 percent have a clothes dryer

More up-to-date Census Bureau data reveals that:

    81 percent have a cell phone

    65 percent have both a washer and a dryer

    58 percent have a computer

According to U.S. Census Bureau estimates (October 2013), 151,014,000 out of a population then estimated to be 306,804,000 (just over 50 percent) received benefits from one or more government programs during the last three months of 2011.

The number of Americans receiving government assistance is greater than the number of those who are working full-time.

In more than 35 states, welfare or government assistance programs provide benefits that pay more than the state's minimum wage. In 13 states benefits exceed $15 an hour, and in 7 states welfare benefits exceed $20 an hour, making welfare recipients' "pay" better than that of teachers and secretaries. In Hawaii, a single mother with two children can receive $61,000 annually in transfer benefits (welfare). That is more than they pay most of their teachers in that state.

Clearly, although labeled as being below the government's constantly rising "poverty line," those living in America whom the government labels as "poor," are living relatively much better off than the government wants us to believe.

When taking into account the availability of and access to good food, healthcare and creature comforts, today's "poor" in America are living better than the middle class did in the 1950s, better than the rich elite in the 1800s, better than the royalty did in the 1700s, and much better than 90 percent of everyone else currently residing on planet Earth. In fact, over 90 percent of the world's inhabitants can only *dream* of having the privilege of being one of America's "poor."

Public assistance has morphed from being a safety net that helps someone to transition *out* of poverty to a system of making people feel more comfortable with just *staying in* poverty. The government even changed from using food stamp coupons to using the pseudo-credit card like the plastic EBT cards, so recipients now just swipe the plastic card at the store to make it appear as though they're using a credit card. Actually it is a credit card, one that is issued and paid for by the taxpayers. Even the name "Electronic Benefit Transfer" (EBT) is so politically correct it almost sounds like they actually earned it.

At the end of the day, welfare programs give the recipients too many reasons not to learn a skill and advance up to the middle class. Federal welfare programs provide a smorgasbord of incentives to remain in the government's poverty trap and under its control.

THE LAW OF EFFECT: INCENTIVES MATTER

As far back as 1898, American psychologist Edward Thorndike conducted animal studies which demonstrated how any behavior resulting in a pleasurable experience will be repeated, whereas any experience resulting in an unpleasant experience is likely to be stopped. He called it "The Law of Effect."

You get what you incentivize. Those who make a career out of legally accepting government "free stuff" are only exhibiting normal, expected human behavior. It is neither just nor fair to judge harshly those who are only guilty of exhibiting the anticipated, normal animal and human behavior.

A 2013 Cato Institute report (*The Work Versus Welfare Trade-Off: 2013*) Tanner and Hughes found that a family of three receiving the maximum government assistance could receive $63,000 in benefits, while an employed worker with a family of three had an average income of $57,000. With today's 126 government programs that disincentivize work, the head of a household of three might think twice before taking a job with a 40-hour work week that pays less than $63,000.

A single parent with two children in the state of Hawaii can obtain a total of $61,000 in federal, state and local transfer (welfare) benefits. So if you have a daughter who plans to go to college to become a teacher to earn an annual starting salary of $30,000 for showing up and working hard every day; our government is incentivizing you to save yourself the $100,000 expense and buy her and the boyfriend of her choosing one-way tickets to Hawaii.

The Economist article "A Memo" (March 1, 2014) reported that currently the U.S. spends less than 20 percent of what other rich countries spend on active labor policies such as job training and work incentives. The vast majority of the U.S. taxpayers' money goes to providing incentives *not* to work.

In *Wealth and Poverty* (2012), George Gilder remarks:

> "The poor choose leisure not because of moral weakness, but because they are paid to do so." [13]

Government programs should be giving the poor the tools (education and skills) they need to pull themselves up to the middle class. Instead, the government sees it to be in its best interest to simply give the poor less reason to achieve and to make them comfortable in their plight. The many people dependent on big government for their food stamps, subsidized housing and free healthcare are essentially required to continue to support those in Washington, D.C. with their votes to keep the "free stuff" coming. You don't bite the hand that literally feeds you, houses you, provides your medical care and even puts the free cell phone in your hand. It's a trap. A poverty trap. It's the dependency that big government wants and needs to grow itself.

The blame clearly rests on the shoulders of the politicians who incentivize the dependency behavior of the voters by continuing to provide positive reward for such behavior for the sole purpose of securing their own political careers.

THE LOST WAR ON POVERTY

In his January 7, 2014 opinion to the *Wall Street Journal*, "How the War on Poverty Was Lost," Robert Rector clearly outlined how the federal government lost sight of President Lyndon B. Johnson's goal "To give our fellow citizens a fair chance to develop their own capacities." LBJ sought to provide "opportunity, not doles." He wanted to increase their ability to support themselves, transforming what he called "tax eaters" into "tax payers" by addressing the causes and not simply treating the symptoms.

LBJ's war on poverty was hijacked by short-term political motives which, instead of providing the poor with opportunities to help themselves, only resulted in making a large segment of them generationally dependent on the federal government.

As President Ronald Reagan often said, "We fought the war on poverty and poverty won."

It's a perfect symbiotic relationship: "You vote for me and you continue to get your Free Stuff." Rather than providing the necessary tools to climb out of government dependency and up into the middle class, the career politicians in Washington, D.C. are simply using free food, free housing, free healthcare and even free phones to buy the votes needed in order for them to stay in power.

When an able-bodied, sound-of-mind adult becomes so profoundly dependent on a government institution for even his or her most basic survival needs, they become a member of the new "victimhood class" or "government dependency class" which approaches a new version of enslavement. The victims are virtually owned by the federal and state governments, which provide their free food, free shelter and free healthcare. The shackles are the 126 government programs that these victims are incentivized to become dependent upon. They have even effectively lost their voting rights by virtue of having to vote for whoever promises to continue to provide the necessities of life they have been made dependent upon.

THE RETIRING POOR

The Baby Boomer generation that shaped America is about to clock out—but not check out—and there lies the problem.

There is an estimated $6.6 trillion deficit between what Americans currently have in savings compared to what they will actually need in retirement, according to an analysis by the Center for Retirement Research at Boston College.

According to the National Institute on Retirement Security, the retirement savings gap is $14 trillion. Only 40 percent of Americans take part in any retirement plan, and the average retirement account balance for U.S. households whose members are age 55 to 64 is only $12,000. The median net worth of the American elderly is about $137,000. When they exclude primary residence, the net worth drops to about $20,000. This puts the next wave of retirees in worse financial shape than their elders, who are already retired and struggling to make ends meet.

Seventy-seven million Baby Boomers are marching toward their retirement with 40 percent having no savings and another 45 percent having inadequate savings for their retirement. Their Plan A and Social Security (the government's Plan A) won't be enough.

But there is a Plan B, and if you are in the top 15 percent having saved more than $300,000 for your retirement, you—the responsible, successful and frugal one—are the government's Plan B. They will need it. The government won't have it. And if you have what is determined to be "more than you need," they will be coming to redistribute it more fairly.

The U.S. Treasury Department already feels entitled to up to 38 percent of the as-yet-untaxed, tax-deferred income in your 401(k), and that will be just the starting point. They know where it is because the banks report it to the IRS. They know how much it is because you report it to the IRS. And without the fanfare of marching troops or rolling tanks, a G-3 level government employee sitting in a cubical can just keystroke it out of your white knuckle, clenched fists and into the Guaranteed Retirement Account (GRA) where it can be fairly and equitably redistributed and administered by the federal government. Do an Internet search for "Cyprus banks 2013." That country is not Russia or China; it is a representative democratic republic with elected leaders.

(Read Chapter 5, "401(k)—They're Coming to Take It Away" for more insight.)

BIG GOVERNMENT

America's Founding Fathers chose a representative democratic republic that stressed checks and balances with the separations of power over a true democracy with a populist government that would almost certainly jeopardize capitalism. Doubters should note the word "democracy" does not appear anywhere in the U.S. Constitution.

The Founding Fathers designed in conditions for gridlock, fearing a system too easily changed would be changed and not for the better. They liked what they had created and they wanted it to survive future self-serving—both left-wing and right-wing—politicians. During the founding of our country's government and the writing of the U.S. Constitution, Thomas Jefferson expressed concerns that are relevant even today:

> "The course of history shows that as a government grows, liberty decreases."

> "Most bad government has grown out of too much government."

> "The democracy will cease to exist when you take away from those who are willing to work and give to those who would not." [14]

THE "JURY SELECTED" CONGRESS

I would like to see those serving in the U.S. House of Representatives chosen by the jury selection system, so we would have more average citizens, selected without regard to political party affiliation, serving for two years making decisions not influenced by re-election concerns. Without the need for campaigning, they could get their work done in half the time, and they would be productive right up until their very last day of service.

If a jury is deemed to be both qualified and suitable for putting fellow citizens behind bars for the rest of their lives or into electric chairs, they should be qualified to handle decisions regarding sweeping healthcare legislation and petroleum pipeline approvals.

THE SOCIAL TIPPING POINT

In his book *Attention Deficit Democracy* (2006), James Bovard states:

"The more people who become government dependents, the more likely that democracy will become a conspiracy against self-reliance." [15]

Great Britain's Prime Minister Margaret Thatcher famously stated, "The problem with socialism is eventually you run out of other people's money."

THE VOTING TIPPING POINT

According to the Tax Policy Center (a joint venture of the Brookings Institution and the Urban Institute), 49 percent of eligible voters pay no federal income tax. Another 11 percent of the electorate paid less than $1,000 annually.

In a democracy there is always a danger that the financially less-productive voting majority, directly or indirectly through those whom they choose to elect, impose taxes for their own redistribution benefit on the unwilling and highly productive minority. The takers outnumber the makers.

In his 1962 book *Capitalism and Freedom*, Milton Friedman states:

"It is very different for 90 percent of the population to vote taxes on themselves and an exemption for 10 percent than for 90 percent to vote punitive taxes on the other 10 percent—which is in effect what has been done in the United States." [16]

In the 1994 classic about the creation of the Federal Reserve, "*The Creature from Jekyll Island,*" G. Edward Griffin remarked:

"When people can vote on issues involving the transfer of wealth to themselves from others, the ballot box becomes a weapon with which the majority plunders the minority. That is the point of no return, the point where the doomsday mechanism begins to accelerate until the system self-destructs. The plundered grow weary of carrying the load and eventually join the plunderers. The productive base of the economy diminishes further until only the state remains." [17]

During the 2012 presidential campaign, a campaign staffer introduced Americans to a fictional character called "Julia" who illustrated the cradle-to-grave welfare system so many American voters had now become dependent on. This caricature was quickly pulled from television advertising because it was realized Americans do not want to look in the mirror and see Julia. Americans didn't want to look in the mirror and realize how dependent on the government so many of them had really become.

H. L. Mencken (1926) in his *Notes on Democracy* wrote:

"FDR's New Deal was the start of the divide of America into 'those who work for a living and those voting for living.'" [18]

THE FUTURE

You can't change the future, but you can be ready for it. If you do the following, it is possible to have a good idea of what the future holds and to be ready when it arrives:

- ▸ Understand the true meaning of assets, liabilities and reversion to the mean and invest in assets—not liabilities
- ▸ Be knowledgeable about the effects of the coming demographic changes
- ▸ Employ the basic tools of Yield Curve, ISM, VIX
- ▸ Always be aware of your current location on the Economic Cycle

Change always brings with it often unforeseen opportunity.

The current trend to watch for is what has been referred to as the "hollowing out" of the middle class. With the Federal Reserve Quantitative Easing (QE 1-4), to the tune of $85 billion a month over the past four years (as of December 2013), most of the money has flowed to the already wealthy. With the dramatic increase in funding for the already existing 126 government assistance programs ranging from food stamps to free cell phones, there is more emphasis on keeping the poor comfortable rather than providing the means and opportunity to allow them to escape their plight and move up into the middle class. That leaves the middle class, which has been completely left out of the recent economic recovery. It is only possible to "hollow out" the middle class up until the following election. They vote. And like any voter, they vote for their best interests.

The economic class evolution of democratic societies follows a predictable path. The large lower economic class model of the 1700s

Fig. 4-1 Economic Evolution of Democratic Capitalistic Societies

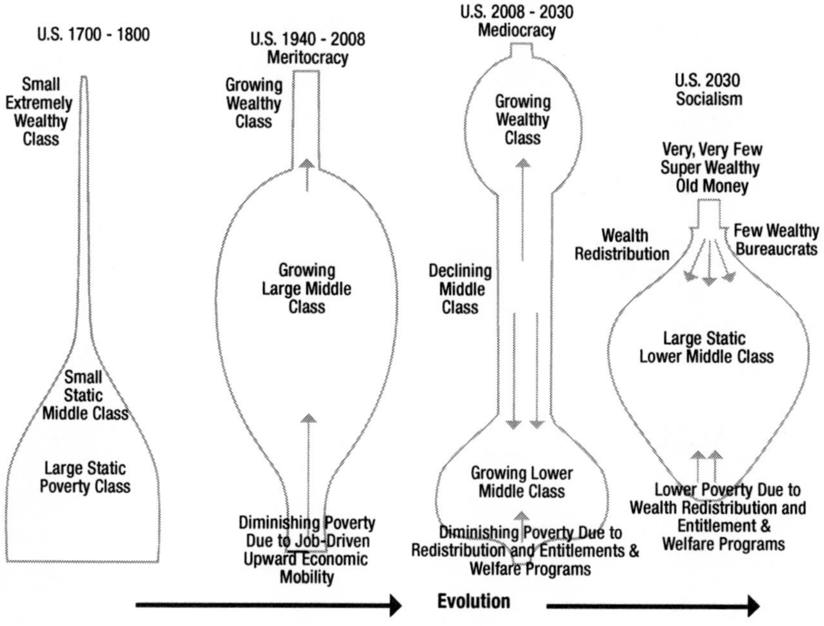

U.S. 1700 - 1800

Small Extremely Wealthy Class

Small Static Middle Class

Large Static Poverty Class

U.S. 1940 - 2008
Meritocracy

Growing Wealthy Class

Growing Large Middle Class

Diminishing Poverty Due to Job-Driven Upward Economic Mobility

U.S. 2008 - 2030
Mediocracy

Growing Wealthy Class

Declining Middle Class

Growing Lower Middle Class

Diminishing Poverty Due to Redistribution and Entitlements & Welfare Programs

U.S. 2030
Socialism

Very, Very Few Super Wealthy Old Money

Wealth Redistribution

Few Wealthy Bureaucrats

Large Static Lower Middle Class

Lower Poverty Due to Wealth Redistribution and Entitlement & Welfare Programs

Evolution

and 1800s evolved to the large middle class model of the 1940s to 2008, which evolved to the hollowing out of the middle class model during 2008 to 2030, which will be redistributed finally into the homogeneous, equality of economic outcome, lower middle class, socialist model (Figure 4-1).

THE SOLUTION

I feel that as a country we need to provide a solution consisting of meaningful education, employable skills, decent job opportunities and personal empowerment. We need to provide the tools and opportunities and not just a handout. As a nation, we should be replacing dependency with opportunity. Free stuff like EBT cards and free cell phones has never helped anyone escape poverty.

We need to help the poor to lift themselves out of poverty. We must not take the easy way out and just settle for making them more comfortable in their poor circumstances just to quell the political unrest.

I believe that each and every American collecting public assistance will gladly trade his or her plight for the pride of a good paying, respectable job. You really do get what you incentivize, so let's incentivize academic achievement, hard work and a life free of the government dependency and control.

Michael Pento, author of *The Coming Bond Market Collapse* (2013) states:

> "I think we need to stop believing in government and start believing in ourselves." [19]

During the 1916 ill-fated Shackleton expedition to the South Pole, the crew witnessed their only ship, the Endurance, be crushed by the Antarctica ice and slip beneath the icy waters.

The old seaman's adage was:

> "Below 40 degrees [latitude, not temperature] south there is no law, below 50 degrees there is no God."

They were way below 50 degrees.

Shackleton commented, "So, now we will go home." [20] Thus they began their harrowing 10-month trek across the ice and back to civilization. Shackleton accepted full responsibility for his situation and took it upon himself to plod along, solving his own problems, neither expecting nor waiting for any aid from the outside world.

Where have all the Shackletons gone? Shackleton and his entire 27-man crew all managed to survive on their own.

SUMMARY

Everybody can't ride in the wagon; someone has to be outside doing the pulling.

It was Karl Marx, author of the *Communist Manifesto*, who stated:

> "From each according to his ability to each according to his need."

There is a current misconception that unequal outcome is the result of an unfair society.

Inequality has always been and always will be all around us: inequality of intelligence, inequality of health, inequality of talent, inequality of ambition, inequality of athleticism. Inequality of height gives me no hope whatsoever of being on an NBA team.

The inequality of income is the result of the inequality of work effort. The top 20 percent of households by income have an average of two employed workers while the bottom 20 percent households by income have an average of 0.5 employed workers—an order of magnitude of 400 percent more employed worker activity in the top earning group. That's the inequality.

Between 1985 and 2004, men with high school educations reported an eight hour increase in their weekly leisure time, while the college-educated men reported a six hour weekly decrease in their leisure time.

Yes, there is inequality of household income and wealth in America, and it is highly correlated with the level of skill and the amount of time and effort those in the household are willing and able to spend working. The top 20% of households, based on income, have an average of 2 full-time workers while the bottom 20% of households have an average of .5 full-time workers—a 400% difference in work effort.

A government cannot give money to someone who it thinks is "deserving" without first taking it from someone who is working.

The U.S. labor participation rate is at a 40-year low because of the 126 federal transfer programs (welfare) designed to disincentivize working. You get what you incentivize.

The lifetime cumulative Social Security benefit for a couple retiring today is over $750,000. Add to that the Medicare and Medicaid benefits and you have the Baby Boomer Million Dollar Entitlement Couple. The Millennial generation is certain to take away the Boomer's punch bowl when they dominate the voting booth after 2020.

Instead of trying to lift citizens out of poverty and into the middle class, the government is creating a poverty trap, where the goal is to make people more comfortable being dependent on the government for their food, housing and healthcare—creating a "government dependency class."

Many studies and experiments have shown that you end up with the behavior that you incentivize. Those who choose to accept the "free stuff" provided by the Federal Government's welfare redistribution programs are only guilty of exhibiting normal and expected human behavior given the incentives and alternatives provided. It would not be "normal" for them to do otherwise. The real blame rests on the shoulders of the politicians who perpetuate the incentives to make citizens dependent on the government to further their own political careers. The poor continue to be stripped of their self-esteem. There is no better way to grow big government than to increase the population that is dependent on that very same government for its food, housing and healthcare.

The vast majority of Americans still want job opportunity more than income equality. That is what has made America great.

When people can vote on issues involving the transfer of wealth to themselves from others who have worked for it, the ballot box becomes a weapon for the unproductive majority to plunder the productive minority. There comes a tipping point where those who work for a living are out-numbered by those who vote for a living.

When the nationalization of healthcare has been completed, nationalization of the existing retirement accounts and their redistribution is next on the federal government's agenda.

Seventy-seven million Baby Boomers are marching toward retirement with 40 percent having no savings and 45 percent having inadequate savings. The only solution is redistribution—robbing Peter to pay Paul... and you're Peter.

If you are one of the 60 percent of those retiring with less than $12,000 saved, you will benefit from the nationalization and redistribution of private retirement plans; because someone else will be paying for your 20 years of retirement. If you are in the top 15 percent having over $300,000 saved for your retirement, *you* are that someone else who will be funding the new plan.

All the more reason to enjoy spending your hard-earned money and dying broke.

As the Dodo said in *Alice in Wonderland*:

"Everybody has won, and all must have prizes."

Don't get angry, get ahead. Put your money into assets instead of liabilities, have an understanding of the effects of the coming demographic changes, and always know where you are on the economic cycle. After you have climbed the net-worth mountain, stop to enjoy the view; then start spending and gifting away every single dollar you earned... and *spend it all.*

CHAPTER FIVE

401(k): They're Coming to Take It Away

Yes they are. They will freeze it, introduce the national program, and then, with a keystroke, move it out of your account and into the scheme before you have time to withdraw it.

This chapter will show you that although a low-fee, properly invested and (un)managed 401(k) plan was a very good forced savings plan, it was saddled with restrictions that did not allow it to be an effective tool for building wealth. Moreover, the planned nationalization of the private retirement programs (401(k)s, IRAs, Roths) will result in the "unnecessarily funded" plans that contain "more money than someone should need to retire" being rolled into some national "Fair Retirement For All Plan" to fund the bailout of all those underwater union and municipal retirement plans that represent millions of votes.

IRA AND 401(k) ACCOUNTS

In 1974, President Gerald Ford signed into law the Employee Retirement Income Security Act (ERISA). This was set up to allow and encourage individual retirement accounts after many people lost their pensions when their employers went out of business. This later led to the 401(k) and other pension plans. It basically put America's employees on notice that employers would no longer be responsible for retired employees and their financial well-being.

The IRA plans became a tax qualified, defined contribution pension plan in 1974. This was followed by the 401(k) in 1978 and the Roth IRA in 1997.

Many in Washington, D.C. see your retirement account not as a responsible, disciplined decision, but as an untapped reservoir of tax deferred wealth they can access to fix the unfunded retirement needs. The American Society of Pension Professionals and Actuaries has set up a website advising 401(k) account holders to tell their elected officials to "keep their hands off my retirement savings."

401(k)—A BAD CHOICE FOR BUILDING WEALTH

These plans provide a good forced savings strategy because of their payroll deduction, the investment of pretax dollars, and the added benefit of employer matching funds. But the majority of wealthy people do not have their money in 401(k) products. They are able to control and grow their wealth more reliably by placing their money into their own businesses, income-producing real assets, and other wealth-building asset classes.

The Roth IRA has the maximum income qualifications of $188,000 for couples and $127,000 for individuals with a maximum annual contribution of only $5,500 (a 6 percent tax penalty for over-contributing) which precludes it as an investment tool for high-income earners looking to build wealth.

As everyone discovered in 1999 and again in 2008, retirement funds in an IRA account or 401(k) are not insured against the inevitable cyclical stock market downturns and losses. And unlike income-producing real estate, these losses are basically gone forever and cannot be carried forward as net operating losses to be used in future years to offset income.

Those who are building wealth expect to continue to build wealth with passive income well after their retirement age. So tax deferred IRA and 401(k) plans are best suited for those who believe their future incomes will decrease and their income tax rates will not increase. They are not the best tools for building wealth.

THE 401(k) FAILURE

It is true that nothing else has promoted more savings by Americans than the 401(k) plan. It is also true that this has allowed workers to amass assets of over $4 trillion in 401(k) and over $5 trillion in IRAs—but at what cost?

The 401(k) plans exposed individual "retail investors" (Wall Street speak for "suckers") to too much risk. In the end, the biggest beneficiaries during both the good and bad economic times have been the enriched Wall Street money managers and mutual fund operators.

In their book *The Little Book of Bulletproof Investing*, authors Ben Stein and Phil DeMuth (2010) state:

> "The 401(k) plan has been an unmitigated disaster for American workers. Here is what we used to have: a defined benefit plan, professionally managed, backed by a rudimentary government guarantee. This was something you could plan a retirement around. Here's what we swapped it for: a defined contribution plan, self-managed (with demonstrably terrible results), high expenses, poor investment choices and no guarantee of anything except chaos." [1]

The IRA and 401(k) plans were a "bait and switch" for the large corporations to allow them to eliminate costly defined-benefit pension plans. Wall Street also liked the idea because they saw that getting their hands on a worker's salary with every paycheck before the worker could spend it elsewhere was a dream come true. It was a perfect scheme: Wall Street managed to get its hands on your money even before you did, almost like having your wages garnished.

The government liked it because it was an easily tracked, growing pot of money that could be taxed when withdrawn in the future at the earned income rates rather than at capital gain rates. Another reason why those in Washington, D.C. like this scheme is because it allows the IRS to keep track of exactly how much money you have in these programs, to know exactly where this money is being kept, and to insure that the money is in an instrument that can be readily taxed or even confiscated with just a computer keystroke. They find this preferable to having you keep your pretax savings in some less accessible instrument such as real estate or under your mattress. Clearly, the IRA and 401(k) plans were a dream come true for the big corporations, the Wall Street money and fund managers and, in the long run, the federal government.

The fees that retirement fund administrators can charge are legendary. Check Appendix 1 to see the 26 possible fees that can be charged to an IRA or 401(k) plan by the administrator:

THE ROTH IRA CONVERSION

The government's "Roth conversions" (tax-deferred account conversion to after-tax Roth IRAs with the associated lump sum earned income tax payment) was a brilliant scheme to grab a big piece of that untaxed money sitting in the 401(k)s.

In 2010 the Federal Reserve's balance sheet was in the midst of a death spiral and the government was in desperate need of a new infusion of tax revenue. The IRS allowed a one-time, "for a limited time only," conversion of an IRA and 401(k) to a Roth IRA without the maximum income restrictions normally imposed ($188,000 for couples and $127,000 for individuals). This allowed the U.S. Treasury to pocket a $600 billion windfall in the first year as poorly advised, hapless souls converted their pretax 401(k) plans into Roth IRA after-tax plans and prepaid a lump sum tax at high earned-income tax rates. The bait the government used was the promise that the after-tax money placed into the Roth account could grow tax free and the withdrawals would never be taxed.

Apparently many financial advisors failed to recall the government's earlier promise to never tax Social Security benefits either (up to 85 percent of a retiree's Social Security benefits can be subject to income tax for couples earning over $44,000). The income tax bill on the money being transferred was over 35 percent for many of the citizens caught up in this scheme who were in the highest income tax bracket. The federal government had conned them into voluntarily sending their big checks to the U.S. Treasury without the unpleasantness of having Congress pass new taxes.

NATIONALIZATION OF YOUR RETIREMENT PLAN

The debt of the nation is massive and almost incomprehensible. "Quantitative Easing" (QE) by the Federal Reserve to the tune of $80 billion a month for four years and counting has increased the money in circulation to the extent that as of October 2013 China is no longer the U.S. government's largest creditor: the Federal Reserve is. And due to 10 years of uncontrolled spending by both political parties, the national debt now exceeds $17 trillion.

The government is in desperate need of money, and it has been eyeing the estimated $11 trillion that is sitting mostly in untaxed IRA and 401(k) deferred tax retirement accounts.

These huge stashes of mostly pretax retirement contributions are in an instrument that the government can monitor; they always know where it is just in case they need to do some politically favorable redistributing to bail out some underfunded union or municipal retirement fund. There will definitely be a need for some type of redistribution to be "fair" to all voters.

If you plan to retire with less than $60,000 in your retirement account, you're in the bottom 85 percent and you're safe. If you plan to retire with more than $300,000 in a retirement account, your account is a target. If you plan to retire with over $1 million, your retirement account has a target painted on it.

Any elected official, if given the opportunity, will gladly stiff the top 10 or 15 percent of retirees with a tax to redistribute retirement money to the other 85 or 90 percent, especially when the top 15 percent represents only 15 percent of the voting public. It will be labeled with a euphemism appealing to the fair-minded, such as "retirement fairness program." Since 2007 the government's working term for this has been the "Guaranteed Retirement Account" or GRA (as in "guaranteed to take your 401(k)").

In 2007, nobody would have believed that healthcare would become nationalized in the U.S., but it is happening. In that case, 85 percent had health insurance, and only 15 percent needed insurance coverage, and the system was still turned on its head in the interest of "fairness" to the 15 percent.

This time around it is the 85 percent who "need it" and the 15 percent who have "more than they should need" for their retirement. As one bill after another comes out of Congress or executive orders come out of the White House, the government increases its control on everything from the food we eat to the healthcare we receive. It should be no surprise that we will be witnessing the confiscation of retirement savings by the forced conversion of private retirement investment accounts into the GRA national retirement account.

IT'S ALREADY HAPPENING: FOREIGN BANK ACCOUNT CONFISCATIONS

It is generally accepted that money is safe in the bank. But when the 2013 Cyprus banking crisis unfolded, it brought about a new reality.

Cyprus, the size of Connecticut, is a representative democratic republic of 1.1 million people in the Mediterranean Sea south of

Turkey. Cyprus is neither China nor Russia; it is a representative democratic republic with rule of law, not unlike the U.S.

In March 2013, over a weekend, all Cypriot bank accounts were frozen. The European Union's plan was to seize (it was called "taxing," like it will be in the U.S.) 9.9 percent of the balance of the insured bank account deposits. The Cypriot Parliament succumbed to the wrath of the voters and unanimously voted this down. Their Plan B was to exempt the insured accounts under €100,000 or approximately $130,000 (the majority of voters) and instead confiscate 47 percent of the wealth in the accounts holding more than €100,000 (a minority of voters). Remember, this was done over a weekend, on frozen private bank accounts in a democratic society with publicly elected officials. It was allowed by the majority of the electorate who were not victimized.

The precedent set by Cyprus is being used as a template for what the governments are referring to as "bail-ins" (solving bank insolvencies with bank deposits as opposed to using taxpayer money, which is called a "bailout"). The government bank deposit feeding frenzy is on.

So your money in the bank is safe as long as the government does not "need it" to solve a bank failure and as long as an unaffected majority does not vote to impose the confiscation on the minority—who they feel have it coming to them.

FOREIGN PENSION FUND CONFISCATION

Now that the European Union, the IMF, and other governments in their feeding frenzy have found they can get away with seizing private bank deposits, they turned their attention to the main course: the trillions sitting in private pension funds.

Iceland: In 2011 the government passed a law levying a 0.6 percent wealth tax on assets in private pension accounts to raise general revenue for the government to fund a job initiative.

Australia: In 2012 the government announced a new 15 percent tax on income over $100,000 drawn from retirement accounts. This is actually a double taxation since the citizens fund their retirement accounts with after-tax dollars much like our Roth accounts, and they had always been told the withdrawals would not be taxed.

Argentina: In 2008 the government seized over $30 billion in private pension funds when they moved private pensions into the government Social Security system for the public benefit.

Portugal: In 2010 the government seized $2.5 billion of private pension fund assets from Portugal's largest telephone company and moved them into the government Social Security system. In 2011 the government confiscated the assets of the four largest banks, consisting largely of private pension funds, to reduce the fiscal deficit.

Hungary: In 2010 the government coerced its citizens to move their $14 billion in the private pension fund into the government fund or risk losing 70 percent of their pension payout from the government.

Bolivia: In 2010 the government nationalized the two largest private pension plans having assets in excess of $3 billion.

Poland: In 2013, in Warsaw, the financial hub of Eastern Europe, the government seized the $37 billion private pension program to reduce a government debt/GDP ratio.

Your IRAs and 401(k)s are designed to be protected investments, but they are not beyond the grasp of the government and its elected officials, regardless of the sovereign nation in which you reside. Rules can and often do change, especially if it is thought to be in the best interest of the public and the majority of voters.

IT'S HAPPENED BEFORE: PRIOR U.S. GOVERNMENT CONFISCATIONS

On April 5, 1933, under President Franklin D. Roosevelt, Executive Order 6102 was issued. Without the prior consent of Congress, the U.S. federal government confiscated gold from the citizens by requiring all "gold coins, gold bullion and gold certificates" to be turned into a Federal Reserve Bank within 30 days. Failure to comply was punishable by a $10,000 fine (a lot of money in 1933) or a 10-year imprisonment or both.

PLANNING THE IRA/401(k) RAID

The nationalization of the retirement programs, including incorporation of (read "takeover of" or "confiscation of") the existing IRAs, 401(k) and Roth IRAs has been quietly building over the past 15 years. The Clinton Administration proposed a one-time tax against the value of private pensions. During an October 7, 2008 Congressional hearing sponsored by the House Education and Labor Committee, pension reform academic professor Teresa Ghilarducci from the New School for Social Research presented a paper introducing her Guaranteed Retirement Account (GRA) program. Her idea was to incorporate the existing retirement accounts and replace future retirement accounts with the government administered program, which will provide retirees with a guaranteed annuity stream annuitized by U.S. treasuries.

In her April 23, 2013 article entitled "Why the 401(k) Is a Failed Experiment" [2], she elaborated on the proposed GRA. This idea has already gained traction. The concept was adopted on the state level in March 2013 when the California legislature passed and the governor approved the legislation to start a Guaranteed Retirement Account system in California.

In 2008, searching for solutions for the economic crisis, the Democratic party caucus led by Senator Charles Rangel and Senator Nancy Pelosi considered the nationalization of 401(k)s, IRAs and other retirement programs to use the assets to "bail out" Social Security. The incentive that was offered was to set the value of everyone's retirement program retroactive to the precrisis values of 2008. This will have appeal to anyone who witnessed the value of their retirement account go down with the stock market and will certainly be revisited during the next stock market downturn.

Senators John Kerry (Democrat – Massachusetts) and Jeff Bingaman (Democrat – New Mexico) introduced Senate Bill S3760 that would require all employers of workers not currently covered by a retirement program to pay 3 percent of compensation into mandatory, automatic IRA accounts administered and controlled by the federal government. It's sort of a Social Security Version 2.0.

A 2010 hearing by the Treasury and Labor departments—presided over by longtime 401(k) critic, Treasury Department Deputy Assistant Secretary J. Mark Iwry—was another effort to nationalize the nation's pension system and to eliminate IRA and 401(k) plans.

During the hearings, a representative of the liberal Pension Rights Center testified that the federal government needs to get involved because IRA and 401(k) plans are unfair to poor people.

The National Seniors Council officials warned that those in attendance wanted the government to require all Americans to buy government annuities (U.S. Treasuries), grab the retirement nest egg of America's most productive senior citizens, and redistribute the wealth of America's older citizens who have responsibly contributed to their voluntary retirement programs most of their lives.

Certain elements of the media are also conspiring. The dramatic cover in the lead article of the October 19, 2009 issue of *Time* magazine called for an end to the 401(k) pension plan, claiming the federal government has an $80 billion per year revenue loss from deferred taxes (it is actually a deferral and not a loss).

The *Atlantic Monthly* November 26, 2012 article "The 401(k) is a $240 billion waste" refers to a Danish study (Danish National Center for Social Research) that recommends doing away with tax deductions for retirement plan contributions because it benefits the rich and is not fair to the poor. They refer to the 401(k) as a wasteful dinosaur for the mostly well-off. Both *Time* magazine and *The Atlantic Monthly* refer to the 401(k) tax deferral as a government subsidy.

> I believe the IRA/401(k) Roth plans were established mainly for the benefit of large corporations, Wall Street money managers and the U.S. government. I also see the benefit of the $11 trillion voluntarily saved, and—so far—untaxed. And if Washington, D.C. wants to set up a new, mandatory retirement program for those who have no retirement savings, well, that's alright too. But what I resent and fear is having the federal government step in and confiscate the existing private retirement savings accounts that hard-working and responsible Americans have worked all their lives to fund. But they will, and it will begin with "If you like your 401(k) plan… you can keep your 401(k) plan."
> I call it the "let's be fair and make everyone equally poor" philosophy.

THE IRA/401(k) CAP AND TAX PLAN

The government is about to decide how much you can save in your retirement account and how "comfortable" your retirement lifestyle should be. The current administration is taking aim at those who save large amounts of money in the tax-advantaged accounts.

In 2014 there was a new proposal to limit the total amount of money an individual can save in the tax-deferred retirement 401(k) and IRA accounts based on the amount needed to finance an annuity that would generate an annual income in the golden years of not more than $205,000. This is the maximum amount of income the government feels you need to have during your retirement years.

With 40 percent of workers not able to take full advantage of the tax-advantaged retirement accounts because they pay no federal income tax, there would be little public objection, and the political consequences would actually be advantageous to elected officials proposing this retirement cap. The only problem is that this cap is just the starting point. The cap will be progressively lowered and the net will be progressively widened to capture all of the upper and middle class taxpayers, just like the Alternative Minimum Tax (AMT) has done.

Another option on the horizon is a European-style Value Added Tax (VAT) on "excessive" withdrawals or a wealth tax on the value of the "excessively funded" retirement accounts in the interest of the public and in the name of "retirement fairness." In his book *The Coming Bond Market Collapse* (2013), Michael Pento states:

> "A VAT tax, a tax of 401(k)s and IRAs and a wealth tax are all areas the federal government may tap to garner additional revenues." [3]

Any and all of the above changes—the cap, the VAT, the withdrawal tax, and a wealth tax on pension plans—would be ushered in under the cloak of Washington, D.C.'s response to an international, domestic, or stock market crisis. The former Secretary of State Hillary Clinton, former White House Chief of Staff Rahm Emanuel and others in DC have proudly stated: "Never let a crisis go to waste."

THE GOVERNMENT'S GRAND PLAN: GRAs

The model for the government's national retirement program, the GRA, was first introduced in its initial version in 2007 at the Economic Policy Institute: Agenda for Shared Prosperity, and published as its Briefing Paper #204.

As mentioned previously, the architect and presenter was Teresa Ghilarducci, the director of the Schwartz Center for Economic Policy Analysis at the New School in New York City, thought by most to be a liberal institution and by some to have a socialist agenda. Her paper titled "Guaranteed Retirement Accounts: Toward Retirement Income Security" was presented at the October 7, 2008 and September 14 and 15, 2010 Treasury/Labor department-sponsored congressional hearings.

> Teresa Ghilarducci's book *When I'm Sixty-Four* (2008), is very informative and very well-referenced with an extensive bibliography. I don't dispute her facts and I admire some of her creative ideas, but I am concerned that her concept will be hijacked and used for unintended purposes to orchestrate a redistribution of the existing large IRA and 401(k) plans to provide the initial funding for the GRA and later to bail out the underfunded union and municipal pension plans.

The GRA plan was to have the value of the 401(k) accounts—diminished due to the 2008, 40 percent stock market correction—revalued back to the pre-2008 stock market decline level and then transferred into individual Social Security-type accounts. Remember the empty "lock boxes?" The government will then invest the money into U.S. Treasury bonds that will yield 3 percent plus inflation and individuals will be required to contribute 5 percent of gross income into these 401(k)s now under government control. By eliminating the 401(k) contribution tax deduction (deferral), the government would expect to increase revenues by up to $240 billion annually. To make up for the loss of the tax reduction to the taxpayer, the government will contribute $600 per year to each person's GRA account.

There have been several variations of GRA plans over the past five years, but the basic concept of taking away an individual's control of their IRA and 401(k) plans and placing them under government control is a common thread. It is called a "transfer" rather than "confiscation" from the individual to the government. They say all plans will be "grandfathered in" at current values but the government will decide when and how much is to be distributed back.

The 5 percent after-tax contribution will be another payroll tax taken from the worker's paycheck each month, along with the continued Social Security contribution. There will be no early withdrawals, no loans from the retirement plans, and when you die the remaining balance will be "retained" (not bequeathed to your family) and redistributed among the other GRA accounts).

The GRA will nationalize and annuitize to U.S. Treasuries so as to invest only in "safe" U.S. government bonds. This is nothing more than a transfer of government risk into government-controlled pension funds. This new annuity will be used to purchase the roll-over of U.S. Treasury debt from the Federal Reserve, forcing government pension funds to become the buyer of last resort of Treasury obligations after China, Japan and others wake up and stop buying the worthless pieces of paper. Requiring the nationalized retirement plan (GRA) assets to be designated exclusively to the purchase of U.S. Treasury bonds seems more like a solution for the Federal Reserve's balance sheet problems than an opportunity for worker retirement savings.

Beware: this is all about funding the $1.5 trillion annual deficits using Americans' retirement money to fund government spending (by buying its Treasury bonds) simply because there is no other remaining pool of wealth able to soak up $1.5 trillion in Treasury bills annually. Just like Social Security, the money will be used to fund federal government spending and will not be put into a "lock box." This will, in turn, allow the government to commence with yet another Ponzi scheme, but this one will be like Social Security on steroids.

This is already starting at the state level. California's Governor Brown has signed SB-1234 (sounds like a fictitious number but it's not), requiring all employers with five or more employees to "contribute" 3 percent of workers' paychecks into CalPERS, the largest pension fund in the country. With this fund already over 40 percent underfunded, this additional payroll tax is nothing more than a thinly veiled, state-mandated bailout of a very badly managed public service workers' pension plan.

The national rollout will come during the next cyclical economic downturn (2018–2020), when the cyclical, coinciding stock market drop decreases everyone's 401(k) values once again by as much as 40 percent (as during the 2000 and 2008 stock market pullbacks). The government will swoop in to solve the real or apparent crisis by revaluing all 401(k) and IRA plans back up to their precrash values, then nationalizing them into GRAs and going forward with annuitizing to U.S. Treasuries. As with any crisis, citizens will be begging for the government to come up with a solution for their problems.

Of course there will be plenty of winners and beneficiaries in this 401(k) nationalization plan. The Service Employees International Union (SEIU) will finally have their right to a retirement both established and fully funded. It will be a windfall for all the underfunded union pension plans. It will be a bailout of the underfunded local and state pension plans. Yes, the GRA plan to nationalize the private IRA and 401(k) plans will benefit many if not most of the voting electorate, but those of us with the top 15 percent of retirement savings in 401(k) and IRA accounts will be picking up the tab.

THE GOVERNMENT'S LATEST SCHEME: THE "myRA"

Announced in January 2014 during the President's State of the Union address, this employer or individually available IRA scheme is designed to provide voluntary participation in a no-fee, tax-deferred plan with an initial investment of only $25 and subsequent monthly contributions as low as $5 per month. Safety is achieved by using only U.S. Treasuries for investment instruments. The plan maxes out at $15,000.

Basically, workers are being asked to loan small amounts of their money to the insolvent U.S. Treasury as a "safe" investment. With an annual return of 1.8 percent (2014) the President is offering workers a safe way to slowly lose money. And these same guys will be running the nationalized retirement programs you will be funding.

THE U.S. GOVERNMENT RAID ON PRIVATE PENSIONS

"Experience should teach us to be most on our guard to protect liberty when the government's purposes are beneficent. The greatest dangers to liberty lurk in the insidious, encroachment of men of zeal, well-meaning but without understanding."
— Justice Louis Brandeis (*Olmsted v United States* 227 US 479 1928)

To be clear, unless there is an IRS lien against you, the U.S. government has no legal standing to seize your IRA or 401(k) retirement accounts. To be realistic, through Congress or by way of an Executive Order, the government could, overnight, freeze and transfer all retirement accounts in the event of a perceived "national emergency." Again, they will not let a national crisis (or an opportunity) go to waste. This is especially true if the goal is thought to be beneficial to 85 percent of the voters.

In his book *Wealth Shift*, Christopher D. Brooke remarks:

> "Imagine how difficult it will be for the IRS to keep their hands off the money sitting in IRAs and other retirement accounts. Tax laws are not biblical laws; they can be changed in response to changing conditions." [4]

The largest source of liquid private wealth in the U.S., $11 trillion, is in private retirement accounts. The ultimate ownership and future control of these funds has been compromised in exchange for the favorable tax treatment of deferred tax payment. The money is not safely locked in a vault with your name on it; it is comingled into a reservoir and put to use by its custodians.

Prior to 401(k) seizures, the trial balloon will be "means testing" of both Social Security and Medicare. This is when the government will tell retired Americans that although they may have paid into both entitlement programs through payroll withholdings throughout their working lives, by virtue of already having "enough," they won't be deemed "eligible" to receive these promised benefits. Not being "eligible for benefits" sounds much better than "not being allowed to receive benefits." If the general public (majority of voters) go along with this Robin Hood rationale, then it is off to the races with means testing for 401(k)s and IRAs.

Next, as a proposed solution to some timely, perceived crisis, the cavalry will arrive on the scene with a nationalized retirement program called the Guaranteed Retirement Account (GRA) using U.S. Treasuries as annuities to protect your money from economic cycle investment or fluctuation of Wall Street investments, and to "guarantee" fair retirement plans to all citizens. This will initially be a voluntary program, but when it becomes obvious that it is vastly underfunded due to a lack of voluntary participation, penalties will be enacted to round up the uncooperative top 15 percent and coerce their participation, much like with the Affordable Care Act.

If you wait until it's a topic on the evening news, it will be too late. The government is not about to watch you terminate and withdraw your retirement savings before they can get their hands on it. Do an Internet search on "Cyprus banks 2013" to see how it is done.

In the event of a government-mandated emergency—probably timed with the next economic down cycle and accompanying stock market fall—regulators will "temporarily freeze" retirement plan terminations and withdrawals in the name of "stabilizing markets." All your retirement money will be "secured" (confiscated) and rolled over into (forced into) the new mandatory national program.

CONFISCATION WILL BE ACCEPTED AND LEGAL

Although many think the confiscation of Americans' retirement accounts is thought to be a "third rail," don't expect this 401(k)/IRA pension fund seizure to be met with the same public outrage as the Affordable Care Act. Remember, the bottom 85 percent stand to gain from this program. The government will receive a $15 trillion infusion of revenue, and trillions of dollars will flow through Washington, D.C. and flood the parched social programs and entitlement programs. Millions will benefit both initially and long term from the bailout by the GRA of the hopelessly under-funded city, county, state and union pension programs. The 60 percent of retirees retiring with no plan and practically no savings will feel like they won the lottery.

As for as the Fifth Amendment, it will be rationalized that the money was not actually "taken" but it was simply "transferred" and "substituted" with U.S. Treasury bonds. There is precedence with other countries having utilized these same tactics.

> When the G-3 employee sitting in his cubicle keystrokes my IRA account information into the computer to redistribute my hard-earned money, the only response he will get is: "Unable to complete transaction due to insufficient funds." My money will be in hard assets that are producing income. I will have a sign on my office door that says "GONE SPENDING."

IT'S NOT TOO LATE

If you do some online research into alternatives to your 401(k)/IRA accounts, you will see that there is no shortage of suggestions. Ideas range from using the money to melt down lead in your garage to make your own bullets, to putting it in an offshore bank you never heard of in a country whose name you can't pronounce.

You should consider the income-producing real estate asset class. You can invest in a single "workforce" market duplex, a couple of small industrial buildings, or a high-rise office complex. If you do your homework and you both understand and follow economic cycles so you know when to enter and exit asset classes—and you do not get yourself overextended—you should do well.

Real estate is not rocket science, although some in the profession might like to think it is. There is a reason why it is called "real property," and stocks and bonds are not. Whatever asset class you choose, just be sure that you're playing your own game and not trying to win at someone else's game.

WHAT'S YOUR RETIREMENT "NUMBER"?

If you watch any of the televised business news broadcasts, undoubtedly you will see ads suggesting that there is a magic "number," meaning a certain value you need to have in your retirement account in order to retire comfortably. But it's not just about the number; it's about the *amount* and *reliability* of the income stream being produced by that number.

> In reality, what you need is a reliable income stream, not just a pile of money. I learned a long time ago that if money was water, I would not want a water tank, a pool or even a small pond... I would just want a year-round, reliable, spring-fed stream running by my mail box.

On the 30th of every month I was broke (I swept my income into investments), but by the 5th I was rich again because the rent from all my business tenants was due by the 5th. Those who paid after the 5th were late and paid late fees, which, to a landlord, is a voluntary 5 percent rent increase or tax the tenant imposes on himself. I know a fellow who named his boat "Late Fee"... guess who paid for it?

If you have income-producing property with no debt service, you can retire with no money in the bank and on the 5th of each month you can be rich and maybe even wealthy. That's a lot better than having a huge nest egg somewhere that makes you break into a cold sweat every time you glance at the front page of your online news source. (I have been told the *Wall Street Journal* is now down to delivering hard copy newspapers to only two people. I wonder who the other one is?)

If weekly earned income is like carrying water in buckets up hill, passive income, from income-producing real estate, for example, is like having a gravity-fed pipe running from the year-round stream to your front door or mail box.

SUMMARY

If your IRA/401(k) plan has a generous employer contribution and the proceeds are invested in an Index Fund with a management fee below .25 percent, you have a reasonably good *investment*.

If there is no employer contribution and the money is invested in an Index Fund with a management fee below .25 percent, you have a good *forced savings* plan.

If there is no employer contribution and your money is being managed for greater than 1.25 percent, you are in a *payroll confiscatory* plan benefiting only the corporation and money managers. You could be doing better on your own, unless you require a forced savings to avoid spending the money.

IRA and 401(k) deferral contribution plans with both Adjusted Gross Income (AGI) maximum phase-out ranges and deferral contribution limits preclude their use by those earning high wages. Since the contributions are deferred and not tax exempted, these plans are for those who expect their tax rates to decrease or their future income to put them into a lower income tax bracket. These are plans designed for those who expect to be poorer in the future, and they are not suitable for those planning to build their wealth.

The well-orchestrated Roth IRA conversion frenzy was a con to provide a windfall for the U.S. Treasury, which was in dire straits. The U.S. will follow the example set by Australia in 2012 and eventually begin taxing Roth IRA withdrawals. Many financial advisors took the bait. Ever wonder why most financial advisors have to get up and go to work every day? (Hint: because they are *not* wealthy.)

Other countries have already begun confiscating bank accounts and retirement accounts. Do an Internet search on the words "Cyprus banks 2013."

In 1933, the U.S. Federal Government confiscated, by Presidential Order and without notice, all U.S. privately owned gold.

The U.S. Treasury began discussions of nationalization of the private IRA and 401(k) retirement plans back in 2007.

After healthcare has been nationalized, the nationalization of private retirement plans is next on the agenda.

Americans between the ages of 55 and 64 have a retirement fund shortfall of over $6.8 trillion or $113,000 per household, and they are retiring at the rate of over 7,000 people daily.

If you have less than $12,000 saved for retirement, someone else will be picking up the tab for your 20-year retirement.

If you have over $350,000 saved for retirement—*you* are that someone else.

Don't get angry, get ahead. You do have alternatives.

You can be ready if you:

- Understand and invest in income-producing hard assets.
- Understand the implications of the coming demographic changes.
- Always know where you are on the economic cycle.

It is not too late to act to spare your 401(k) or IRA from being confiscated and redistributed, so that you can enjoy *spending it all*.

CHAPTER SIX

The Coming U.S. Default

This chapter will show you why you need to have your retirement money in hard assets and under your own control. This is the only way you will be able to go to sleep every night knowing that when you awake you will still have the money you earned and saved, so that someday you will be able to *spend it all*.

"The budget should be balanced;
the treasury should be refilled;
public debt should be reduced;
and the arrogance of public officials should be controlled."
— Cicero, 106–43 BC

PIMCO (Pacific Investment Management Company) founder and manager Bill Gross calculates that the U.S. debt is not just the $17 trillion (2013) outright liability, but is actually $75 trillion when the contingent liabilities of Social Security, Medicare and Medicaid are added in, as any private company would be required to do. The underlying assumption that governments do default on pension promises is the main reason why the government does not include the contingent liability of present-day value of future pensions in the reported debt-to-GDP ratios.

WHAT IS DEFAULT?

Default has both time and value components.

Historically, a debt was in default if it was unilaterally not paid on or before the agreed-upon date, or if it was paid with money or any instrument having a lesser present-day value. Countries printing their own currency routinely escape the real burden of debt through inflation and the subsequent devaluation of the currency. The Federal Reserve target of 2.3 percent annual inflation allows a 30-year U.S. Treasury bond to be paid back at maturity at a rate of only several pennies on the dollar when valued in terms of purchasing power. Today few would consider this to be a technical default.

PRIOR FOREIGN DEFAULTS

Putting technical defaults aside, a major sovereign default is the refusal or inability of a government or sovereign state to pay its debt in full and on time.

In their book *This Time Is Different* (2009), Carmen M. Reinhart and Kenneth S. Rogoff reported that between the years 1800 and 2009 there were over 250 sovereign external defaults on foreign-held public debt and over 68 cases of sovereign internal defaults on domestically held public debt.

Iceland defaulted in 2008 when Icelandic banks held debt valued at more than six times the country's GDP and ended up defaulting on over $85 billion. The Icelandic currency plunged, decreasing the disposable income of its citizens by 18 percent. Iceland chose not to spend tax dollars on bailouts. Unlike the U.S. "bailout and borrow more money" approach, Iceland admitted the truth, defaulted on the debt, said they were sorry, and started anew.

Iceland's approach was to allow the banks and private enterprise to take their losses and to re-establish capitalism as an economic model rather than to do a bailout and socialize losses at the expense of the current taxpayers and future generations. As a result of their conscious decision to "frontload" the pain (as opposed to passing it on to the next generation), they are further along in this economic recovery with a 3 percent growth rate.

PRIOR U.S. FEDERAL DEFAULTS

The U.S. defaulted on its debt in 1790, 1933 and 1971, and experienced monetary defaults in 1792 and 1876. [1]

America was born in default. In *This Time Is Different*, the authors note that soon after the Revolutionary War, the New Republic was in arrears on $11,710,000 in Foreign and Domestic Debt when the U.S. Treasury agreed to accept the states' debts.

The first secretary of the Treasury, Alexander Hamilton, defaulted on this debt when he paid the creditors less than what they were owed and borrowed more money to put the new Republic in a more solid financial position. The U.S. deferred interest payments on the debt issued by the new Federal Government until 1801.

John Chamberlain at the Mises Institute argued (2011) that the U.S. defaulted on Continental Currency in 1799, domestic debt in 1782, greenbacks in 1862 and Liberty Bonds in 1934.

FDR's 1933 DEFAULT

In 1933, in the midst of the Great Depression, the U.S. again defaulted on its sovereign debt related to the repayment of its prior gold-based obligation.

U.S. bonds, including those issued to finance America's expense in World War I, as well as the previously and currently issued currency, provided the holders with an unambiguous promise that the U.S. government would give them the option to be paid in gold coins or bullion. The "Gold Clause" was standard in debt contracts of that time. This assured that bondholders would be protected against depreciation of paper currency by the government. Nobody doubted the clarity of the "Gold Clause." On June 5, 1933 Congress, along with the urging of President Roosevelt, passed a Joint Resolution repudiating the government's obligations and leaving the bondholders with only the depreciated paper currency provision.

The resulting lawsuits ended up in the U.S. Supreme Court, which upheld, by a vote of five to four, the government's refusal to honor its promise to repay in gold.

PRESIDENT NIXON CLOSES THE GOLD WINDOW

On August 15, 1971 President Richard Nixon, unilaterally and without prior congressional approval, issued Executive Order 11615 suspending direct dollar-gold convertibility, thus preventing foreign Central Banks from redeeming U.S. currency for gold as had previously been agreed upon in the 1944 Bretton Woods Accord.

While not strictly a default on a U.S. debt obligation, by unilaterally deciding to no longer allow U.S. dollar-gold convertibility, the U.S. government abdicated a financial commitment it had made to the world.

What was to be known as the "Nixon Shock" brought the final end to over 2,500 years of commodity (actual gold or silver) money and fiduciary (currency and coins backed by silver or gold convertibility) money and ushered in fiat (nonprecious metal-based and only changeable into other denominations of itself) money backed by faith. With the inscription "In God We Trust," the U.S. dollar was no longer "good as gold." It has been said "we traded gold for God."

RESERVE CURRENCY DEFAULTS

It is often said a government with debt denominated in its own currency (reserve currency) technically should never have to default because it can print (or electronically create on computer balance sheets) more money to pay the debt. Thus is the luxury of having a currency of a fiat money and not a commodity or gold-backed currency. Just the same, Russia, Ecuador and Jamaica have all defaulted on their own currency debt within the past 15 years.

U.S. DEBT: ABBREVIATED VERSION

As of February 2014, the U.S. has approximately $17 trillion in government debt. Five trillion dollars is held by government and related agencies such as the Federal Reserve Bank. Of the remaining $12 trillion, roughly half or $6 trillion is held domestically by banks, mutual funds, retirement funds and individuals. Six trillion dollars is held by foreign nations with China holding $1.3 trillion and Japan holding $1.2 trillion. The Federal Reserve alone holds over $2 trillion worth of debt, making it a larger holder of U.S. debt than either China or Japan. These holdings have increased by over 400 percent since 2008 due to the Federal Reserve's Quantitative Easing (QE) bond purchases to orchestrate low interest rates and a failed Keynesian attempt to stimulate the economy.

Contrary to popular belief, the Federal Reserve does not "print" more money to purchase these treasury bonds. It actually "keystrokes" digital or electronic money out of thin air and enters it electronically into the balance sheets of the Federal Reserve accounts of U.S. banks. The printing presses only operate to replace the damaged currency estimated to have been lost from circulation.

INFLATION = CURRENCY DEVALUATION = DEFAULT

The "keystroke" creation of digital electronic money increases the money supply and devalues the currency. The Federal Reserve has long declared its target of 2.5 percent annual inflation, which is a 2.5 percent annual decrease in purchasing power and in turn, a 2.5 percent annual devaluation of U.S. currency.

This means those who loan money to the U.S. government by purchasing U.S. Treasury bills or bonds will be paid back in currency that is decreasing in value and purchasing power at a rate of 2.5 percent annually. Investors who bought 30-year U.S. Treasury bonds in 1946, experienced an average 2 percent annual decrease in their purchasing power for a cumulative, real inflation-corrected 91 percent loss of the principle's purchasing power. Paying back debt in a currency that has been devalued—to the extent of losing 91 percent of its purchasing power—would be considered by some to be a default on the initial loan, because it is being paid back with a currency of less value and purchasing power.

The U.S. inflation rate was 20 percent in 1880, 20 percent in 1918, 18 percent in 1947 and 14 percent in 1980. William McChesney Martin, Federal Reserve Chairman from 1951 until 1970 often said, "Inflation is a thief in the night." John Maynard Keynes said this about inflation: "By this means government may secretly and unobserved, confiscate the wealth of the people, and not one man in one million will detect the theft." [2]

In *End This Depression Now*, author and 2008 Nobel Prize winner Paul Krugman makes his case for the government's intentional inflation and outlined three benefits of higher inflation, including the decrease in real value of debt by allowing the debt to be paid off in lesser valued, cheaper dollars. He concludes: "The reality is that inflation is actually too low." [3]

Historically, it should be noted that the Roman government dealt with their increasing debt problems by diluting the amount of silver in the coins down to 5 percent, at which time the coins became worthless. Before the Romans, the Spaniards created inflation by shaving silver off the edges of the coins to devalue coinage. This led to the practice of adding ridges to the edges of coins to show which coins had not been devalued by shaving.

The Chinese have an issue with our Federal Reserve's stated 2.5 percent inflation target. Guan Jianzhong, president of Dagong Global Credit Rating Co., Ltd.—the only Chinese agency that gives sovereign debt ratings—has said: "In our opinion, the U.S. has already been defaulting." He goes on to say the U.S. has already defaulted on its loans by allowing the dollar to weaken against other currencies, lessening the wealth of all creditors including China. The Federal Reserve can drag down short-term interest rates globally by holding short-term rates in the U.S. low with monthly purchases of $8 billion in treasuries, a scheme it euphemistically called "Quantitative Easing" (QE) or, as the Federal Reserve prefers "expansion of the monetary base."

> One of the reasons I like income-producing property is that both the income stream (rents) and the value of the underlying assets (real estate value) are basically indexed to inflation, so over the long term, purchasing power is retained despite the orchestrated devaluation of the U.S. currency.

FUTURE DEFAULT?

Insidious default through inflation and currency devaluation only delays the day of reckoning, at which time actual default is the only option. The great majority of sovereign nations have crossed this threshold at least once.

PIMCO's cofounder and manager Bill Gross has been ringing the alarm for a few years. In his 2011 corporate newsletter he addressed the almost incomprehensible math of total U.S. entitlement liabilities on a discounted (they will continue to climb higher) net present value basis. He goes on to state:

> "Unless entitlements are substantially reformed, I'm confident that this country will default on its debt; not in conventional ways, but by picking the pocket of savers via a combination of negative real interest rates." [4]

Bill Bonner and Addison Wiggin, authors of *Empire of Debt*, (2006) state:

"The U.S. dollar bills in Japan are used to buy another form of U.S. paper, Treasury bonds. The U.S. can print as many hundred dollar bills as it wants. So can it issue as many bonds and notes as it pleases. As long as people don't try to exchange them for other forms of wealth, all is well." [5]

In *USA Inc.*, Mary Meeker, the former Morgan Stanley top analyst, reviewed the U.S. finances as if the country were a corporation. She reports the unadvertised, unrecorded and unpublished debt of the U.S., when the "off balance sheet" liabilities are added in, is an actual debt burden of close to 500 percent of GDP [6]. Her hypothetical analysis has been received with high praise by former Federal Reserve Chairman Paul Volker, investor and former New York City mayor Michael Bloomberg and a host of others.

In *The Clash of Generations: Saving Ourselves, Our Kids and Our Economy* (2012), author and Boston University economics professor, Lawrence Kotlikoff calculates that to eliminate the Federal Government fiscal gap would require either a 64 percent increase in all federal taxes or a 40 percent cut in all federal expenditures.

So the basic tools available to the government in the short term are:
(1) Higher inflation to allow the debt to shrink in future dollars
(2) Currency devaluation with a decline in the dollar's value
(3) Treasury yield suppression to minimize the interest due on the outstanding debt

The elephant in the room that everyone seems to be ignoring is the immutable economic law of "reversion to the mean" as it relates to the interest rate on the national debt. It is like the law of gravity is to astronomers. There is a reason why it is called the "mean"—that is where the value averages out to be over time. With the current two-year Treasury bill at 0.37 percent and the 10-year Treasury at 2.6 percent (April 2014), with both facing mean values of 5.9 percent and 6.6 percent respectively, the cost of U.S. debt is on a collision course with reality.

In *End This Depression Now* (2013), author Paul Krugman states:

> "Governments depend on being able to roll over most of their debt, in effect selling new bonds to pay off the old ones. If, for some reason, investors should refuse to buy new bonds, even a basically solvent government could be forced into default." [7]

> "Could this happen in the U.S.? Actually, no. The Federal Reserve would step in and buy federal debt, in effect printing money to pay the government's bills. Nor could it happen to Britain or Japan or any country that borrows on its own currency and has its own central bank." [8]

> "In fact, it would not be a tragedy if the debt actually continues to grow, as long as it grows more slowly than the sum of inflation and economic growth." [9]

Dr. Krugman goes on to correctly state that the $241 billion in debt the U.S. government owed at the end of World War II (120 percent of GDP at that time) has never been paid off and there is no plan in place to do so.

> I don't see today's children or grandchildren ever writing checks to pay off this huge, growing federal debt. The only reality is default. The "D" word will never be used, of course, except by the countries we stiff by paying the common sovereign default settlement of 30¢ on the dollar. You'll see innocuous, smokescreen euphemisms like "debt restructure," "debt reorganization" or "settlements."

A small debt is not a problem for either the borrower or the lender.

A large debt could become a problem for the borrower.

A really huge debt is really a problem for the lender, not the borrower.

This reality came to light during the 2008–2010 home mortgage loan crisis, when millions of borrowers walked away from their home loans, leaving the lenders with most of the big losses.

Once the U.S. debt crossed the $1 trillion threshold, our debt to China and Japan became *our* embarrassment but *their* problem.

Probably the U.S. will clandestinely trade Taiwan to China (pontificate and bloviate, but look the other way and not fire a single shot when China invades Taiwan) in return for a 70 percent write-down of the U.S. debt they are holding.

Bonner and Wiggin (*Empire of Debt*, 2006) addressed the issue of unpaid debt:

> "When people cannot pay their debts, they do not pay them. But the debt does not cease to exist. They are merely 'paid' by someone else—the creditor." [10]

To make matters worse, in the 19th and early 20th centuries the U.S. government and American citizens borrowed to invest and produce. Now consumers borrow to consume, and the U.S. federal government borrows to unproductively redistribute. Investment debt is self-liquidating, while consumer debt is self-debilitating.

In *The Real Crash*, author Peter Schiff is decidedly pessimistic:

> "There is no way American taxpayers can repay the money the federal government has borrowed. That means our creditors are going to have to take huge losses... So either we default or we allow inflation, but honest repayment isn't an option. Given a choice between the two, default is by far the better choice, even for our creditors." [11]

STARVE THE BEAST

The only way to curb runaway federal government spending might be to "starve the beast." With the top one percent of taxpayers providing over 51 percent of the federal income tax revenue, just the top one percent of earners could decide to earn just the average annual salary of $50,000 and go on vacation for two years, basically cutting up Washington, D.C.'s credit card. If just the top one percent of earners, who pay over 51 percent of the federal income tax revenue, were to quit work (remember, they can afford to quit) and pay no taxes for three years, America the Great would be back in the Stone Age: no social programs, no entitlements, and no military defense force. You might think twice before pissing off that top one percent.

THE [*your name here*] ECONOMY

Among all this doom and gloom of past and future defaults, there is good news: the preceding has been about other financial defaults... not yours. At the end of the day, it is only what happens in the [*your name here*] economy that really matters.

When building your wealth, it is important to keep your focus on the ultimate prize: financial independence through safe, reliable, steady, passive income. You will need to stay focused.

Of course it is important to be aware of current events so you are not operating in an information vacuum, but it is equally important to filter out information that is not relevant to achieving your goal. Reading the headlines and brief summaries found in the *Wall Street Journal* (the U.S. interpretation) and the *Financial Times* (the European interpretation) online will give you 99 percent of what you need to know to follow the economic cycle. The rest is just noise. Your brain box's hard drive has a fixed capacity, so put up a good "financial spam" filter.

Be concerned only with what you have control over: balancing the [*your name here*] budget, keeping the [*your name here*] debt under control, and controlling the [*your name here*] economy.

SUMMARY

In 40 BC, Cicero complained about problems with the national debt and about not having a balanced budget. Nothing is new; it's just forgotten history.

Default is the unilateral failure to pay a debt on time with an instrument having the same present-day value.

There is a long history of foreign sovereign defaults on both debt and currency, both in the U.S. and around the world.

The U.S. has a history of both past and ongoing territory, state and municipal defaults. America was born into default, and one of the first actions of the new U.S. Treasury was to default on outstanding U.S. debt obligations.

The U.S. Federal Government has defaulted three times on its debt and twice on its currency.

The Federal Reserve's stated 2.5 percent inflation goal is an annual 2.5 percent devaluation of the currency and just a slow-motion, ongoing default.

The Federal Reserve is now the single largest holder of U.S. national debt, not China or Japan.

Once the U.S. debt owed to China and Japan crossed the $1 trillion threshold, it was large enough to become the lender's problem, not the borrower's. China is still buying our debt only because it's their first rodeo. Someday they *will* wake up.

You need to only be aware of, anticipate and avoid any negative consequences of national and international policies and events. If it is beyond your control, don't let it waste your time and emotional energy. You don't have to like it, but you do have to accept it. Deal with it. Move forward. Don't get angry, get ahead.

Remember, it is only the [*your name here*] economy that really matters. You only need to concern yourself with balancing *your own* checkbook and servicing *your own* debt obligations and building *your own* wealth. The rest is just "noise." Avoid the distractions in life. As long as you are able to keep the [*your name here*] economy from going off the tracks, you will be able to build wealth, protect it from being redistributed by the government and look forward to... *spending it all.*

PART III
ENJOY YOUR WEALTH

CHAPTER SEVEN

Lifestyle: You Have Choices

WEALTH IS RELATIVE

In *Stone Age Economics* (1972), author Marshall Sahlins reviewed early reports of the 1940s scientific expeditions that studied the primitive societies still in existence at that time in Australia. She made note of the ways to achieve relative wealth: the wants can be satisfied either by producing more or by needing or desiring less.

> I believe happiness does not have to be the result of one's circumstances. Happiness is a choice, and regardless of your impoverished or extravagant circumstances, you are the one who ultimately chooses to be either happy or unhappy.
>
> Today's concept is that man's wants are great or maybe even infinite, whereas his means are limited. The Zen version of affluence—where human wants are few and means are adequate—can lead to contented people with a low standard of living. It is the "want not, lack not" theory of personal contentment.

In a primitive society, the roving hunters must carry all the comforts they possess, and so they only possess what they can comfortably carry themselves. For the primitive hunters, possessions were a burden; thus they had no desire for possessions and maintained an undeveloped sense of property ownership. What we see today as being poor, primitive man saw as being free.

WORKING HOURS IN PRIMITIVE SOCIETIES

In his classic *Economic Anthropology* (1958), author Melville J. Herskovits lived within and studied the ongoing primitive Bushman society and concluded that hunters and gatherers worked less than we do today. They had much more leisure time, and there was a greater amount of napping during the day than in most modern societies. He observed the average length of time per person per day spent appropriating and preparing food was four or five hours, and that was not continuous work.

In *Kung Bushman Subsistence: An Input-Output Analysis* (1969), author Richard Lee noted the average daily per capita subsistence yield for the Dobe Bushman was 2,140 calories. With the estimated daily caloric need per capita estimated to be 1,975 calories for their physically undemanding economy, these primitive societies were not on the verge of starvation and in fact had enough food left over to feed their pets.

PRIMITIVE SOCIETY WORK FORCE PARTICIPATION RATES

Lee also found that in the primitive hunter/gatherer, prefarming societies, 61 percent of the people were effective food producers, with the remaining being too young or too old to contribute. In another primitive culture that he studied, he found 65 percent of the people were effective contributors to food acquisition. His ratio of food producers to the general population was 3:5 or 2:3. He also noted that the working 65 percent still only worked 36 percent of the time and the remaining 35 percent of people did not work at all.

PRODUCTIVITY IN PRIMITIVE SOCIETIES

Lee estimates that in primitive societies, even the producing individuals had 4.5 to 5.5 days a week available for leisure activities. They worked about 15 hours a week or an average of two hours and nine minutes per day.

While researching for his paper *An Introduction to Hadza Ecology* (1968), the author James Woodburn observed primitive societies over the period of a year. He found that individuals spent on average less than two hours a day obtaining food. The rest of their time was spent sleeping, talking, gambling and visiting within their own or nearby groups of people.

MODERN TIMES: YOUR "LIFE ENERGY" and "WORK, TIME AND EFFORT"

In *Your Money or Your Life* (1991, 2008), authors Vicki Robin and Joe Dominguez state: "Money is something we choose to trade our life energy for. Our life energy is our allotment of time here on Earth, the hours of precious life available to us. When we go to our jobs we are trading our life energy for money." [1]

> I read *Your Money or Your Life* in 1995 and I have the updated 2008 edition on my "review annually" bookshelf. The two figures in this chapter are from that book.

EARNED IOUs

Is important to consider what you are trading away with your many hours of work. I like to think of the "life energy" in more concrete terms of "work, time and effort" and go one step further by converting the "work, time and effort" into "earned IOUs," which are given to you in the form of physical money or electronic money, a string of 1s and 0s, deposited in your bank account.

In either the physical form or electronic form, this "money" by itself serves no purpose. It won't satisfy your hunger, keep you warm and dry, or provide enjoyment. This money is just an IOU given to you in exchange for your "work, time and effort."

But the "earned IOUs" can and should be converted into what satisfies your hunger, keeps you warm and dry, and provides you with enjoyment—what I call "Fun Stuff."

The number of earned IOUs you need to trade your life energy for is determined by what you feel you really need and for what you are willing to trade your "work, time and effort."

> One day I woke up to realize that I had traded a lot of my "life energy" or "work, time and effort" piling up my earned electronic IOUs that I might never get to convert into enjoyable Fun Stuff. I decided I was not going to allow my earned, electronic IOUs to be taxed and redistributed by the government to strangers who chose not to put in their own "work, time and effort."
>
> I needed a plan.
>
> I needed a good plan.
>
> I needed a good plan to convert it all into both voluntary gifting and Fun Stuff... that is what the last chapter is about... *spending it all!*

THE "FULFILLMENT CURVE"

In *Your Money or Your Life*, authors Robin and Dominguez illustrate that a certain level of earning is needed to survive, a higher level is required to achieve comfort, and a still higher level is simply "enough" (Figure 7-1). This concept, called the Fulfillment Curve, is very important to understand. The authors go on to say:

Fig. 7-1 The Fulfillment Curve: *Enough*

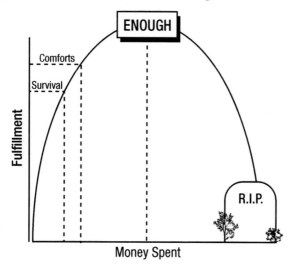

Robin & Dominguez *Your Money or Your Life*, 2008

"The word is 'enough.' At the peak of the fulfillment curve we have enough: enough for our survival, enough comforts, and even enough little 'luxuries.' We have everything we need; there is nothing extra to weigh us down, distract or distress us, nothing we've bought on time, have never used and are slaving to pay off. Enough is a fearless place." [2]

In college I was at the bottom of the "fulfillment" curve where I had few expensive wants and I was able to trade off very little "work, time and effort" to achieve them.

At the peak of my career I was at the top of the spectrum, where my lifestyle was expensive to maintain. I spent huge amounts of "work, time and effort" for the "earned IOUs" that I rapidly depleted by converting them into what I thought were necessities and Fun Stuff. As I was rocketing to the sky—leaving the "enough" point of the Fulfillment Curve in my rear view mirror—my girlfriend told me "success is getting what you want, but happiness is wanting what you have," as she walked out the door... and out of my life.

Later in life I became aware of the difference between putting my money into assets rather than liabilities, and I became more fiscally responsible. I found myself needing fewer "earned IOUs," but I still forged ahead, working hard and trading my "life energy" for more and more "earned IOUs." As the Europeans have long said, they work to live while Americans live to work. I was guilty as charged. I let these earned IOUs pile up in their electronic form and, from time to time, converted them into income-producing assets, mainly real estate, for my early retirement.

FINANCIAL INDEPENDENCE: BEYOND THE "CROSSOVER POINT"

The concept of financial independence is best expressed as Robin and Dominguez did with their "crossover point" illustration, shown below in Figure 7-2.

As you decrease your monthly expenses and increase your monthly passive income, you will eventually reach a crossover point where the passive income rises above the falling or plateaued expenses [3]. Beyond this point is the ultimate freedom: financial freedom and true wealth.

Being "rich" usually means making a lot of money and needing to spend a lot of money. It is like being on a treadmill.

Being "wealthy" is having enough passive, unearned income to allow you to enjoy the lifestyle you have chosen without the need to spend any more of your "life energy" or "work, time and effort" to maintain it.

Fig. 7-2 The Crossover Point

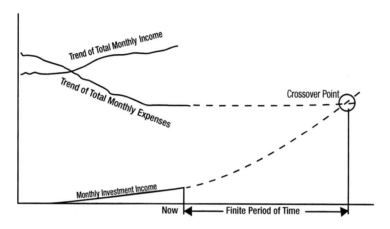

Robin & Dominguez *Your Money or Your Life*, 2008

"Rich" is a treadmill. "Wealth" is financial freedom.

SUMMARY

In the 1940s, studies of the then still-existing primitive hunter/gatherer societies in rural Australia revealed that primitive man was a slacker by today's standards. He was able to meet his needs and wants by working an average of two hours and nine minutes a day. He took "weekends" that lasted three or four days, and spent much of his time napping, playing games and socializing. We can only imagine what they would report if they studied the average American worker's daily and weekly activities. He might conclude that society had *changed* but not necessarily *advanced*.

When you go to work, you trade your "life energy" and use your "work, time and effort" to earn money.

"Money" itself has no use. The physical (cash) or electronic (bank deposit) forms are simply IOUs you earn that can be converted into life's necessities, into Fun Stuff, or given to someone else who may or may not earn it.

Your "work, time and effort" earns enough money first for survival, then for comfort and finally to achieve "enough" to be happy (Figure 7-1). You might be satisfied with "enough" or you may continue to spend your "work, time and effort" to achieve more than "enough"—maybe to the detriment of your lifestyle.

Building wealth involves raising your passive income while holding level or lowering your expenses. When your passive income curve crosses your expense curve, you have reached the "crossover" point and you are now enjoying and building wealth (Figure 7-2).

"Rich" is earning and spending large sums of money without building net worth.

"Wealthy" is having enough passive income to enjoy the lifestyle you aspire to live and to still build your net worth without having to apply your own "work, time and effort."

"Rich" is a treadmill. "Wealthy" is financial freedom.

You build wealth by putting your money into income-producing assets, understanding the implications of demographics and always knowing where you and the economy are positioned relative to the economic cycle.

That hyphen between those two dates on your gravestone is not very long... so you need to get started now, regardless of your age.

Procrastination is the thief of time.
— Charles Dickens

CHAPTER EIGHT

Enjoy Your Wealth
and Spend It All

"Twenty years from now you will be more disappointed by the things you didn't do than the ones you did. So throw off the bowlines. Sail away from the safe harbor. Catch the trade winds in your sails. Explore. Dream. Discover."
— Mark Twain

Steel magnate and philanthropist Andrew Carnegie, builder of the New York City library, famously said: "He who dies rich, dies disgraced."

Now, let's get going. After all, in two days, tomorrow will be yesterday.

If you have spent a good portion of your life learning a skill while others played, working while others slept, putting your money into assets while others were buying "stuff," you are probably sitting on a nice pile of your hard-earned money or net worth.

DELAYED GRATIFICATION

By practicing delayed gratification (putting your money into assets rather than liabilities), you will be able to build wealth rather than just be rich. But some of us have become prisoners of our own delayed gratification—the very same traits that have made us successful—to the extent where we toil away and delay gratification to our own detriment.

The challenge you will face will be if and when to suddenly reverse course and start redeeming all those electronic IOUs by spending them to buy Fun Stuff or for gifting.

Your money in the bank or brokerage accounts is just electronic money, a series of ones and zeroes, provided to you for your work, time and effort. At some point in time you will need to decide if you're going to leave them to someone else, let the government redistribute them, or convert them into Fun Stuff and gifting for your own enjoyment.

THE FAMOUS WHO DIED BROKE

If you die broke after having led a financially successful and respectable life, you will be in good company.

The following U.S. presidents died penniless:

Thomas Jefferson

James Madison

James Munro

William Harrison

Ulysses S. Grant

James Garfield

Harry S Truman (he and his wife were also the first two recipients to enroll in President Johnson's Medicare Program).

THE "DIE BROKE" PHILOSOPHY

Baby Boomers are reinventing retirement. The Baby Boomers' parents, the Greatest Generation, measured their life's success by how much money they left to their children. Today's Baby Boomers measure their life's success by how much money they spend on themselves.

Some people may be offended by the notion of "spending it all" rather than leaving some money behind for others. The unforeseen and often tragic consequences of leaving a lot of money behind after one's death—with only written instructions and often limited oversight—are legendary. It reads like a Who's Who of lottery winners five years after the fact, but with the added drama of emotional family theatrics and attorneys billing by the hour. If you feel the need to give your money away, do it before you die so you can be sure of where it goes and how it is used—and personally experience the satisfaction. Sometimes the best gift one can leave behind is nothing for the grieving family to fight over.

I first read about Stephen Pollan's and Mark Levine's book *Die Broke* in a 1995 *Worth* magazine article [1]. *Die Broke* (1997, 2005) [2] and their *Live Rich, Die Broke* (2005) were early inspirations and they remain on my book shelf today.

The "die broke" theory advocates building wealth in life. But whereas traditional estate plans seek to preserve assets up to and even beyond one's life, most die broke proponents advocate converting one's liquid and illiquid assets into insurance policies and guaranteed streams of income. They focus on the Income Statement rather than the asset and liability Balance Sheet. Assets are converted into an income stream with the purchase of an annuity, and into insurance with the purchase of long-term care insurance or other insurance tools.

In *Die Broke* the authors list seven financial tools: annuities, long-term care insurance, disability insurance, major medical insurance, term life insurance, reverse mortgages and charitable giving. They are often quoted as saying, in jest, that your last check should be written to the undertaker, and the check should bounce.

You can't help but notice that six out of the seven financial tools involve handing over your hard-earned money to an insurance salesman. Do you really want to do that?

When you buy an annuity, you are giving up control of your capital. Annuities are virtually irrevocable due to their high penalties. They might not keep pace with inflation, insurers pay large commissions to the producing agents, and they are only as certain as the financial solvency of the insurance company.

With an annuity, the insurance company from which you buy the policy might not be the company you will be depending on for the income stream. Highly rated insurance companies have been known to sell annuity units to lower rated insurance companies. The insurance companies take the upfront payment you make for the annuity and invest it in stocks, bonds, commercial mortgages and real estate. Those funds have the same vulnerable exposure to the market's cyclical fluctuations as all the other Wall Street investments. The state-owned insurance company guaranty funds do not have even close to the reserves necessary to cover major losses, and states have a maximum insured amount ranging from between $300,000 and $500,000. If you die before receiving the full monetary benefit of the annuity, the remaining balance is retained by the insurance company.

A lot of very bright people spend a lot of time, money and computing power to build actuarial tables, which the insurance companies use as a guide to construct the annuity and payout schedule to virtually guarantee that some of the initial principal (purchase price) plus investment earnings will be left over for their shareholders. Their legal, primary fiduciary responsibility is to their shareholders, *not* the policy holders.

There is an advantage to the Pollan and Levine version of *Die Broke*, which is really "die annuitized and well insured." By liquidating assets and handing over the proceeds to the insurance companies in the form of six of their seven financial tools, you will never have to worry about not having insurance or an income stream. You will never really "die broke" or spend it all before you die.

In their book *Spend 'Til The End* (2008), Boston University professor Laurence J. Kotlikoff and Scott Burns provide good, insightful, conservative advice to the mainstream retirement crowd. They advocate a solid plan of consumption smoothing. The Pollan/Levine and Kotlikoff/Burns approaches probably achieve the comfort level sought by most people.

Build Wealth & Spend It All is not about handing over your hard-earned money to an insurance salesman for annuities and a long-term care insurance policy. This is about deciding to take control and beginning a responsible and systematic plan for you—not someone else—to get the satisfaction and enjoyment from every cent you have ever earned.

> Every time I fly into a large city I see that the tallest and grandest buildings bear insurance company names. They were built with money that came largely from the unrealized future income streams of policyholders. Each proverbial brick in those buildings represents someone's work, time and effort, which they chose to give to an insurance company rather than spend on themselves or their loved ones.

REVERSE MORTGAGES

Here, again, the insurance companies win. Seldom is the cashout greater than 70 percent. The fees can be onerous, and again, the actuarial tables greatly favor the insurance companies. It would be better to gift the house to someone in the family, either directly or via a trust, or to just sell it and enjoy gifting or spending the money.

YOUR LIFE IS A HYPHEN

While my University of New Hampshire classmates were flying to Bermuda or Daytona Beach for spring break, I was back at my familiar job at the Wyoming Cemetery just north of Boston. I never did get a good answer as to why they called it the "Wyoming" cemetery.

While working summers mowing and trimming grass, I noticed the tombstones, grave markers and monuments all had an etched date followed by a hyphen, which, in turn, was followed by another date. I realized my life experiences would forever be represented by just a hyphen—and only I would know how great that hyphen really was. I never forgot that revelation, and later in my life, after having rocketed way past the "enough" point on the Fulfillment Curve, I decided I was going to make that one hell of a hyphen.

My gravestone will have a date of birth, a date of death, and a hyphen in between. During that hyphen, I will have both earned and enjoyed spending or gifting my entire big pile of my net worth.

I'm not afraid to die broke because that's how I started. I am more afraid to die watching my hard-earned money and electronic IOUs taken from me and handed to some stranger against my wishes.

MY TIME-TRAVEL PERSPECTIVE

To put what seem to be major decisions into perspective, I sometimes use the "time travel" perspective.

I close my eyes and envision that I'm an old man in a nursing home. I picture myself sitting in one of those old, high-back wheelchairs, probably with a seatbelt restraint, surrounded by other elderly, drooling old folks staring off into space in a room with a muted TV that no one is watching. I ask myself the question: "If I were to do it all over again, what would I decide to do? What do I now wish I had done at that time in my life?"

I have found this to be a great way to put what seem to be major decisions into perspective.

THE PLAN TO *REALLY* "SPEND IT ALL"

To get on this train you need to be at the point where you are Balance Sheet wealthy but no longer Income Statement obsessed.

The commission-based insurance salesmen and TV pundits ask you: "Do you want to outlive your money?"

You need to ask yourself: "Do I want my hard-earned money to outlive me?"

Your money should not outlive you. It should be used for your benefit and the benefit of your loved ones. Every dollar left behind after you die is a dollar—not to mention your "work, time and effort" spent earning it—wasted. When you have climbed the mountain and reached your peak net worth, don't forget to enjoy the view.

Life does not have a reset button.

Involuntary impoverishment is a terrible way to live and die.

Here's a better way: voluntary, strategically planned, semi-impoverishment, very late in life. First experience the thrill, enjoyment and satisfaction of piling up a respectable net worth, then enjoy converting every last cent into Fun Stuff or gifting—now that's the way to both live and die.

Voluntary, strategically planned, permanent self-impoverishment is not for the faint of heart. It requires both discipline and courage: the discipline to earn and build wealth by applying the "work, time and effort," and the courage to be willing to convert it all into Fun Stuff and meaningful gifting while still alive.

You need to accept that you will not be buried in the fanciest casket, in the most expensive plot, at the classiest cemetery. You have to be able to live (and die) with that decision.

Some of the best advice about retirement financing is given thousands of times each day by airline attendants:

> "If the oxygen masks fall from overhead, first put on your own oxygen mask, then assist those next to you."

If you can't take care of yourself, you will not be of any help to others. This is true with personal finances.

In his book *The Great Crash Ahead* (2011), Harry S. Dent recalls a conversation he had with his child's godmother:

> "I should have spent it," she said. "Instead of socking it away, meeting with my financial advisor on a regular basis, and tweaking my investments, I should have blown it all on the vacations I wanted to take. Even though I was responsible, saving and paying my own bills, never spending beyond my means, I'm suffering for it. Other people blew up their own situation... And I'm here paying the price." [3]

I aspire to end my life in voluntarily, strategically planned, and diminished circumstances with great memories which cannot be unwillingly redistributed to strangers in the name of "fairness."

I plan to be the guy in the nursing home with the greatest memories and the least money.

I would rather be broke and have rich memories than be rich and have broken dreams.

I do not expect my family members, business associates or friends to accept my "spend it all" philosophy, but I have finally moved beyond existing just to seek the approval of others.

I just tell them that I have never seen a hearse with a luggage rack.

Life is not for sissies, and neither is dying broke.

THE "CONVERTING CURVE"

I call it the Dying Broke Converting Curve, as in converting your past "work, time and effort" (net worth) into meaningful gifting and Fun Stuff (Figure 8-1).

Fig. 8-1 Dying Broke Converting Curve

Solvent (not destitute) – a leveraged, mortgaged income property provides end-of-life final cash flow

But

Broke – the income property value = its debt service + outstanding consumer debt. You get to spend all of your earned wealth without stiffing anyone (including the undertaker).

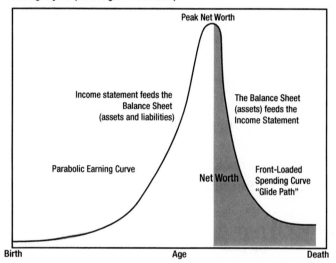

By applying your "work, time and effort" to building a big pile of net worth, you slowly climb this curve. Technically, this is a process of using your Income and Expense Sheet to build up your Asset and Liability Balance Statement. It is also the curve you will rapidly descend by converting your earned net worth into Fun Stuff or gifting it to deserving people while you are still alive. Technically, you deplete the positive balance on your Asset and Liability Balance Statements to feed your Income and Expense Sheet. Here's how:

First you set up the parameters of the Conversion Curve, based on your age, life expectancy (see the actuarial table in the appendix), and amount of net worth. Next you decide on the spending curve, which has both time and magnitude. Finally, you decide where to safely "park" your net worth so it does not suddenly and unexpectedly disappear before you have enjoyed spending it on Fun Stuff or gifting it. It is important to have your net worth in a safe place because the plan is to die broke…not live broke.

Going from left to right along the X axis, you progress up the curve by applying your work time and effort to building a pile of assets called net worth.

Assigning a date for the peak and determining the degree of downward slope is determined for each individual by age, health, gene pool, life expectancy, and one's tolerance of being broke before being dead.

Moving down the right side of the curve you will convert your assets and net worth into both Fun Stuff and voluntary gifting to the deserving individuals of your choosing while you are still alive.

To put it more technically, you will be using your Asset and Liability Balance Statement to feed your Income and Expense sheet until the Balance Statement zeroes out. At that point you will be insolvent and technically broke. By keeping the last, mortgaged, income-producing property, you can still be liquid and have spending money, because your cash-on-hand (an asset) could equal your last mortgaged income property outstanding mortgage (a liability). You will be insolvent, technically broke, but still liquid and not destitute.

When you die, the cash-on-hand will pay off the outstanding mortgage so you will not only have spent everything you earned in life, but you will also have paid all off your bills, including the prepaid funeral expenses.

Your last a check to the undertaker will *not* bounce.

Don't stiff the undertaker.

My Own "Converting Curve"

Here's the process I used for constructing my own Converting Curve:

(1) I established in the Y axis and labeled it from zero to my anticipated maximum net worth five years from now at the age of 68.

(2) I labeled the X axis with my age starting with birth at zero and ending at age 88. I would need a crystal ball to be completely accurate of course. However, by using an actuarial table and factoring in other variables such as my biological parents' age at the time of their natural deaths, my health over the past 64 years, my lack of unhealthy habits, the environment in which I live, and my relatively safe (boooooriiiing) lifestyle—I can add a corrective factor to the average statistics and come up with an anticipated end-of-life in 27 years rather than the 19 years stated in the actuarial tables. Okay, so maybe it's just a little better than a wild guess, but at least it is a starting point. The curve is a living document that can be continuously modified, either accelerated or delayed, as determined by life's circumstances.

(3) Next I chose the peak net worth inflection point of the Converting Curve. The ascending wealth-building curve represents my accumulation of real assets and bank account electronic assets (net worth) starting with zero at birth (no trust fund there) and maxing out at age 68. Note that this curve is not linear because it is similar to, though not identical to, compounding interest: building wealth is usually parabolic and not linear. Successful wealth builders really do disproportionately accelerate their rate of accumulation of wealth over time.

I chose age 68 for the top or inflection point of the curve because it allowed me to maximize net worth while still leaving enough time to enjoy spending it. If I wanted to start my spending curve earlier (and I was willing to settle for less net worth), I would have moved the inflection point both lower and further to the left to a younger age. Like everything in life, it's a trade-off. If I were to develop a serious health issue tomorrow I would surely move the inflection point all the way to the left to my current age and immediately get onto the spending curve.

I chose to spend more time building up a larger net worth so I can enjoy a more dramatic and memorable gifting and spending experience. Some choose to only build up a small net worth pile and start spending earlier in life and more modestly.

> I consider life to be like the rides in an amusement park. Some people are content to sit in the "tea cup" ride—leisurely, slowly and safely spinning around. I prefer to get in the first car on the biggest rollercoaster in the park and endure the long, unexciting trip up that first steep hill. Then, just when the "clicking" stops, my knuckles turn white as I hold on for dear life and scream my lungs out while plunging to what seems to be certain death.

Finally, I drew the down slope portion, or the "Spending Curve" starting at the inflection point of maximum net worth and ending at zero. Note that I chose a parabolic and not a linear downslope. This reflects my plans to front-load the spending schedule and have my greatest spending year at age 68, the second greatest spending year at age 69 and so forth, with my lowest spending year being at age 88. At age 68 I have many more options and much more stuff to spend money on than I'll have at age 88… a gold-plated walker or diamond-studded cane?

MONTE CARLO SIMULATION

I'm working on a Monte Carlo computer simulation program to make my Converting Curve dynamic rather than static and both more flexible and more accurate in real time.

This computational algorithm is used for the optimization and generation of samples from a probability distribution, thus allowing the construct of a model with many changing input variables. In this case, the input variables of changing age, passive income, remaining principal, spending, economic cycles and health can be updated and entered to turn a static and outdated curve into an updated and almost real-time dynamic curve.

Note that I decided to leave a time period from the time of going broke to the time of dying. If I live until age 96, like my mother, I will spend eight years in the nursing home. Unlike my private paying mother, I will be a Medicaid patient. But I will have a smile on my face because I will always be able to close my eyes and have both great memories and the satisfaction of having both built a small fortune and having spent every single hard-earned dollar the way I chose to. I'm willing to live (and die) with that trade-off.

SPENDING MODE: TIME AND MAGNITUDE

As comedian Henny Youngman used to say: "I have all the money I need... if I die by 4:00."

At this point in life, there should be no need for successful wealth builders to generate more income, so they have no need for annuities. As a wealth builder you do not want to lose control of your net worth irreversibly by placing your capital into the hands of strangers while you are still alive. Your concern should be scheduling the harvesting of your wealth so you neither outlive your harvest nor die leaving your large net worth crop rotting in the field.

SPENDING HAS BOTH TIME AND MAGNITUDE
Time:

In two days, tomorrow will be yesterday, so don't wait until you are older than God's baby pictures before you start spending. It's a lot more fun converting money into Fun Stuff at age 68 than age

88. There is only so much gold plating that can go on that walker and so many diamonds that can be attached to that cane.

Magnitude:

The magnitude of the Fun Stuff or gifting depends on the size of the accumulated net worth. It's just as simple as that.

Someone with a very large net worth might buy yachts, planes or a tropical island retreat. They can also underwrite a new wing for the local hospital or renovation of the city museum, or fund an academic building at their alma mater.

Someone with a smaller net worth might consider purchasing a bigger boat, a nice vacation house, or a luxury car that was always thought of as being too expensive. They might also want to fund a Habitat for Humanity house to help change an entire family's life, fund a grandchild's higher education to put them on a promising path in life, or help out an elderly relative.

Someone with a more modest net worth might want to buy an RV and travel, buy a classic sports car, or start dining out at the restaurants previously thought to be too expensive. They might also want to make a donation to their favorite charity or church, help out the local Meals on Wheels, or buy a plane ticket allowing a relative away at college to be home for Christmas.

> My mother always had ugly slipcovers on the nice furniture to protect the upholstered arms from wear and to protect the fabric from direct sunlight. When she was 90 years old and wanted to downsize, we sold the beautiful furniture that had been so well protected. The new owners carried off the furniture and left the slip covers behind.

I remember my father having cheap, plastic seat covers protecting the nice, original upholstery in his car. When he sold the car, he removed the seat covers, exposing the beautiful original upholstery for the second owners to enjoy.

I have always put floor mats in my car, regardless of the season, to keep the original carpeting looking like new to increase the resale value.

At some point in life it just makes sense to stop covering the furniture upholstery, car seats and floor carpeting so they can be enjoyed by you instead of the next owners. You should enjoy it during your lifetime and let the next owners cover the faded upholstery, worn car seats and stained floor mats to hide the wear and tear evidence of your use and enjoyment.

In the spending phase you give yourself permission to remove the slipcovers, seat covers and floor mats.

RESPONSIBILITY

The Greatest Generation's greatest fear was running out of money and ending up in "the poor house." I still remember hearing the admonishment, "If you don't shut off the lights you will put us in the poor house." They saved and even hoarded their money with a Depression-era mentality.

Dying broke isn't for the fearful or insecure.

It is a real and present fear. It's clearly not for everyone. It's a leap of faith that your memories of how much you enjoyed spending all of your earned net worth will be more satisfying to you than the thought of the nursing home bill being paid through automatic withdrawal from your trust account instead of by Medicaid.

The "spend it all" philosophy is voluntary impoverishment where people who have worked hard to accumulate significant assets make a conscious decision to cash in their earned net worth for Fun Stuff and gifting while still alive. It's enjoying the fruits of your labor before it is redistributed by the federal government to others who somehow feel they are entitled to it. It is a personal decision to be made by only you and your spouse and for only yourselves. You have no right to voluntarily impoverish someone else, such as a spouse. Most people would agree that taking your own (financial) life, like suicide, should not be a criminal offense, but taking someone else's financial life is a capital offense. Dying almost broke is a couple's decision, but dying really broke will most often be a decision left up to the surviving spouse.

> I know my father would not have wanted to die and leave my mother destitute, but I believe he would have preferred that she spend their last hard-earned dollar doing what she and they enjoyed rather than unwillingly and unknowingly having a nursing home siphoning it off while she napped.

I do not advocate intentionally dying in debt. Debt does not go away; it becomes the creditor's losses. Some have made the case that the difference between dying with $200,000 in the bank and dying with $200,000 in debt is $400,000 of fun. Although I advocate spending everything you have earned, I do not advocate spending what others have loaned to you in good faith.

Your last check should *not* bounce.

Don't stiff the undertaker.

Another consideration would be if there were an impoverished, elderly relative or a child who was financially dependent due to a physical or cognitive disorder, precluding their employment or financial self-sufficiency.

For most average people, the best plan might be the conservative, traditional retirement strategy of starting with a portfolio of stocks, bonds, and cash, then proceeding at a 3 or 4 percent annual withdrawal rate. But, if you were "average" you would not be reading this book and you certainly would not have made it to this page.

> I don't plan to smooth or even out my spending; I plan to frontload my spending to a period of time where I can enjoy my spending the most. Rather than smoothing my consumption, I'm strapping in, holding on tight and riding this roller coaster right to the bottom... white-knuckled and screaming all the way.

GIFTING

Fun Stuff can involve more than just spending on yourself. One of the greatest advantages of having accumulated wealth is having the ability to positively change someone else's life. A good example of this is Michael Zitz's *Giving It All Away: The Doris Buffett Story* (2010), which documents the quiet philanthropy of Warren Buffett's sister.

With premortem gifting, you can enjoy giving to your choice of deserving individuals or charitable causes while you are still alive to enjoy the pleasure and satisfaction. You can gift to your children when they really need and can most benefit from your generosity, whether it is for their education, their wedding or their first house, rather than having them receive the gift by default when you die and they are middle-aged adults. While alive, you can control the amount, the timing and the outcome of your generosity better than you can from the grave by leaving behind a document for your heirs to contest and their attorneys to manipulate.

SAFELY "PARKING" YOUR WEALTH

You might not be able to take it with you, but you want enough to get you there.

While you're on the spending side of the Conversion Curve, you will want to protect your precious, hard-earned assets and earned net worth. You will no longer be looking for a return *ON* capital, but rather, a return *OF* capital.

Your first goal will be to keep it safe. If you can keep the principal safe and still add incrementally to your net worth with passive income, the more there will be in the pile to be converted to Fun Stuff or gifted.

Wealth can be held in three asset formats: printed currency, electronic assets and real assets.

(1) *Printed Currency Assets:* The folding money in your wallet is labeled "Federal Reserve Note," which is a debt to the Federal Reserve and not the U.S. government as were the previously issued United States Notes (1862–1971). They are not backed by gold or silver as were Gold Certificates (1863–1933) or backed by silver as were the Silver Certificates (1878–1964). It is imprinted with "legal tender" which only means it has to be accepted in the U.S. for domestic monetary transactions and to settle debts. "UNITED STATES OF AMERICA" appears in print but with only an implied U.S. government guarantee. The Federal Reserve Note in your wallet is fiat money having no intrinsic value and is no longer redeemable in, or backed by, gold or silver. And finally it is imprinted with "IN GOD WE TRUST" but don't count on him backing it either.

(2) *Electronic Assets:* These are the assets you see on your brokerage or bank statement or website that indicates the value of your stocks and bonds or the cash balance in your bank account. It is just a string of 1s and 0s on a computer that can be easily manipulated—as illustrated by the Bernard Madoff scandal—or deleted by a Russian teenager sitting in his cold basement who is keystroking your identity away.

(3) *Physical Assets:* The best example of a physical asset is income-producing real estate. It is not just a coincidence that the first word in "real estate" is "real." It will work for you 24 hours a day, seven days a week. You can go to bed at night knowing that when you wake up it will still be there. Property rights are some of the most enduring rights afforded to U.S. citizens.

Gold is more of a fear commodity with very limited practical use. It is a currency without a country. It is difficult to safely store, difficult to easily move, and it does not pay rent or dividends.

In an apocalypse, you can't eat it, you can't defend your family with it and it won't run your generator. As soon as you take it out in public to trade, you and your family will become targets. Betting on the world's ending has been a losing bet for over 65 million years. The only future value of gold is the hope that someone else, more scared and less intelligent, will come along and pay more for it.

The following are two financial instruments where you can park your net worth so it will be both accessible and reasonably secure. No financial tool, bank or mattress is completely safe. The only time you will not have to worry about losing your money is after you have already spent it all.

TIPS

Treasury Inflation Protected Securities or TIPS have been around since 1997, but they're not very exciting. They have low yields but also low risk and a high safety factor. They did have a slightly negative return briefly during the Great Recession. In their book *Risk Less and Prosper* (2012) authors Zvi Bodie and Rachelle Taqqu provide an excellent brief and comprehensive review of TIPS. Some would recommend a "bond ladder" if liquidity is not of paramount importance.

INDEX FUNDS

For those of you who think you can beat someone else at their own game, index funds are the safest, most profitable and, for most people, the only way to play the Wall Street equities game. Only a few managed mutual funds, such as Berkshire Hathaway, have beaten the Standard and Poor index funds in the long run.

The father of this asset class is John C. Bogle, author of *The Little Book of Common Sense Investing* (2007) and numerous other good books on managed index funds.

While a student at Princeton University, Bogle made mutual funds the subject of his senior thesis. After being fired as CEO of the Wellington Fund he started his own company, The Vanguard Group. In 1975 Bogle started the first retail index mutual fund benchmarked to the Standard and Poor 500. Initially referred to as "Bogle's Folly," it is now one of the world's largest mutual funds, known as the Vanguard 500 Index Fund. After a successful 1996 heart transplant, John Bogle returned to Vanguard as the senior chairman.

In 1999 *Fortune Magazine* named Bogle one of the four "Investment Giants" of the 20th century, and in 2004 *Time* magazine named him one of the world's 100 most powerful and influential people. The following are some of his often quoted comments:

> "History confirms that the best strategy for investing in the stock market is to own all of the U.S. publically traded companies in a long-term portfolio, without the risks of frequent trading and with the lowest management fees possible. This is what an index fund is all about. It is a fund that holds many stocks chosen to mimic the overall performance of the overall market. This eliminates the risks of individual stocks, market sectors and manager preferences."

> "The other hallmark of the unmanaged index fund is the very low management fees of less than .25 percent compared with over 2.5 percent for some managed funds."

In his book *Enough* (2008), Bogle states:

> "Thus, while investing in American business is a winner's game, beating the stock market before those costs is a zero-sum game. But after intermediation costs are deducted, beating the market—for all of us as a group—becomes a loser's game." [4]

In his book *The Little Book of Common Sense Investing* (2007), Bogle remarks:

> "But the costs of playing the investment game both reduce the gains of the winners and increase the losses of the losers. So who wins? You know who wins. The man in the middle (actually, the men and women in the middle, the brokers, the investment bankers, the money managers, the marketers, the lawyers, the accountants, the operations departments of our financial system) is the only sure winner of the game of investing. After the deduction of the costs of investing, beating the stock market is a loser's game." [5]

Bogle goes on in his book *Enough* to recant a story often told on Wall Street, of the investment banker addressing his colleagues after the collapse in the mortgage-backed bond market:

> "I have bad news and good news. The bad news is that we just lost a ton of money. The good news is that none of it was ours." [6]

Bogle quotes Charles T. Munger, Warren Buffett's partner at Berkshire Hathaway, who puts it this way:

> "The general systems of money management [today] require people to pretend to do something they can't do and like something they don't. [It's] a funny business, because on a net basis, the whole investment management

business together gives no value added to all buyers combined. That's the way it has to work. The poor guy in the general public is getting a terrible product from the professionals." [7]

Bogle often remarks that the mutual fund (401(k)) investor puts up 100 percent of the money, takes 100 percent of the risk, and gets only 20 percent of the profit, if any, only to pay income tax at the capital gains income tax level.

Another proponent of index funds, Burton G. Malkiel, the Princeton University professor and author of *A Random Walk Down Wall Street* (1973, 2012) states:

"Investors would be far better off buying and holding an index fund than attempting to buy and sell individual securities or ostensibly managed mutual funds." [8]

Malkiel provides an example:

"An investor with $10,000 in 1969 who purchased shares in the average actively managed fund would have seen his investment grow to $258,000 by 2010.

"If the same investor had invested $10,000 into a Standard & Poor 500 Index Fund, by 2010 he would've had a portfolio worth $463,000—an 80 percent or $205,000 advantage of the S&P Index Fund over the average actively managed mutual fund." [9]

Warren Buffett, the second richest man in America, has on numerous occasions stated that his best two personal investments have been the farm land he purchased years ago and the building he bought in New York City... both real estate assets. He has also made public (Feb 29, 2014 Berkshire Hathaway 2014 Annual Letter to Shareholders) that in his Last Will and Testament he is leaving cash to his wife with instructions for their financial advisor to put 90 percent of it into a Vanguard S&P 500 Index Fund. That pretty much settles it as far as I'm concerned.

STOCKS FOR THE *REALLY* LONG RUN

Unfortunately, most individuals know very little about how their 401(k) money is being invested. All too often, we hear of the "buy and hold" philosophy popularized by Wharton School professor Jeremy J. Siegel in his popular book *Stocks for the Long Run*. (1994, 2014). What is referred to as "average stock market return" is an average that works out over a 50-year period—a *really* long run for most investors. But if your investment timeframe falls into one of the 10–20 year periods with no growth, the long-term average stock market returns will not be much of a consolation to you. Even Warren Buffet's legendary Berkshire Hathaway has had four periods of 40% or greater losses since 1962.

If you had invested in the stock market in 1929, you would not have regained your losses until 1952. If you had been in the market from 1967 to 1976 you would have seen no increase in your stock values. If you had been in the market in 1999, it would have taken until late 2013 for you to regain your losses when correcting for inflation (unless you were invested solely in the NASDAQ, in which case you would still be waiting to get back your original investment). If you were holding dividend-paying stocks you would, at least, have some consolation.

Financial advisors often recommend investing for the long term in well-diversified portfolios of stocks, bonds and mutual funds. Diversification is not a viable strategy for building wealth. It is just a plan to minimize risk. Diversification is a good strategy if you have no idea what you're doing and you don't have the time or are not willing to make the effort to figure out what you should be doing. Warren Buffett's commonly quoted opinion about diversification is:

"Diversification is a protection against ignorance. It makes very little sense for those who know what they are doing."

Clearly, a low-fee index fund is the easiest and safest way to invest in the stock market, but it is not a reliable tool for building wealth. How many people do you know personally who retired wealthy by investing in the stock market, as opposed to starting a successful business or investing in income-producing real estate?

THE BLINDFOLDED MONKEY STOCK PICKERS

Burton Malkiel, an economics professor at Princeton University and the former head of their Economics Department, is the author of the classic investing book, *A Random Walk Down Wall Street,* which advocates the efficient market hypothesis and makes a good case for index funds over managed funds.

Malkiel hypothesizes that share prices move completely at random, making the stock market entirely unpredictable. In his book he makes the now famous statement:

"A blindfolded monkey throwing darts at a newspaper's financial pages could select a portfolio that would do just as well as one carefully selected by experts." [10]

Testing the hypothetical dart-throwing monkey theory in 1998, the *Wall Street Journal* began the first of many dartboard stock picking contests. In the first contest, *Wall Street Journal* staffers threw darts at the *Wall Street Journal* stock page while investment experts picked their own stocks. After six months they compared the results of the two methods. Initially, the experts edged out the darts, but over time the experts fared less well against the dart throwing staffers.

A team from Research Affiliates in Newport Beach, CA published a study in the summer 2013 issue of the *Journal of Portfolio Management* [11] that used both a computer-simulated dart throwing monkey and an inverted or reversed stock picking strategy to beat a market capitalization bench mark 96 out of 100 times.

In several studies, live monkeys were recruited into the dart throwing contests. The following live monkey experiments and some human stock picking competitions were reported by Partners4Prosperity.com [12]:

(1) In 1999, a chimpanzee named Raven threw 10 darts at a dartboard of 133 Internet-related companies. Within six trading days, one of her random choices was up 95 percent. By the end of the year Raven's portfolio of 10 randomly selected stocks had outperformed more than 6,000 Internet and technology money managers earning an astonishing 213 percent return.

(2) In 2010 Circus chimpanzee Lusha's international portfolio topped 94 percent of Russia's managed mutual funds, nearly tripling her initial capital of 1 million rubles ($35,884). Pavel Trunin, the head of Russia's monetary policy at the Institute for the Economy in Transition responded: "It shows that financial knowledge does not play a great role in giving forecasts to how the market will change."

(3) In the *Wall Street Journal*'s 46th Investment Dartboard Contest of 2012, the darts again beat *Wall Street Journal* readers' picks, as they have over 60 percent of the time since 1988.

I believe there will be a proverbial sucking sound as the Baby Boomers sell out their stock positions to raise cash for their retirement. The Millennials who watched the 1999 and 2008 beating taken by the retail investor Baby Boomers, will say "Thanks, but no thanks" to Wall Street.

With the goal of achieving a return *of* capital as opposed to a return *on* capital after you have already built your net worth, it is best to be content with just parking your liquid net worth in the two financial instruments of TIPS and index funds and your illiquid net worth in income-producing real estate.

> When *my* will is read it will begin with the statement: "Being of sound mind and body... I spent it all."

Once you have built your wealth, don't spend too much of your precious time over-thinking what you are going to do with it.

"The greatest enemy of a good plan is the dream of a perfect plan."
— Prussian military theorist Carl von Clausewitz on *War* (1832)

"Everyone has a good plan... until he gets punched in the face."
— Mike Tyson, boxing champion

SUMMARY

Your money in the bank or brokerage account is just a series of computer code: electronic ones and zeroes. It is an IOU you earned for providing work, time and effort that had value to someone. You only redeem their value when you convert these IOUs into Fun Stuff or gifting. Your earned IOUs not converted to Fun Stuff or gifting represents your uncompensated "work, time and effort."

Seven former U.S. presidents have died broke, after having both earned and enjoyed spending their wealth.

Most "die broke" proponents advocate the purchase of numerous insurance products and the conversion of assets into an income stream with the purchase of annuities. This will only result in your dying over-insured, leaving a portion of your net worth to an insurance company. You will never actually get to enjoy spending or gifting every dollar you have earned and subsequently, you will not actually be dying broke.

The "Conversion Curve" illustrates how you climb the net worth hill by building wealth and then descend down the other side, converting your hard-earned net worth into Fun Stuff and gifting while you are still alive.

The upward-sloping wealth building curve should be almost logarithmic, with the occasional, inevitable, brief, financial setbacks.

The net worth inflection point is determined by how high you want to build your earned net worth and how long you are willing to wait before starting to spend it.

The downhill spending curve should be parabolic so that spending is frontloaded to occur at a time when you will still be young and healthy enough to enjoy spending it. Don't wait until you are older than God's baby pictures before you start to enjoy spending your hard-earned net worth, unless you want to have the only gold-plated walker in the nursing home.

The final end point at the bottom of the curve can be planned so you end up with modest means: insolvent, technically broke, but not destitute.

Dying broke after having applied work, time and effort to build a comfortable, positive net worth, is a personal, conscious, strategic, and irreversible decision that must be made by both consenting adult spouses. To do otherwise would be irresponsible.

After having built up "enough" wealth, it is important to stop putting your capital at risk and to "park" it in a relatively safe but liquid financial instrument, such as TIPS or a Vanguard Index Fund. You want to *die* broke... not *live* broke

In two days, tomorrow will be yesterday... so get started!

A Final Word

Y ou *can* build wealth.

You *need* to protect your 401(k) from government redistribution to bail out underfunded municipal and union retirement programs.

You *deserve* to spend or gift every dollar you've earned while still alive.

You *do* deserve to... *spend it all*.

Building wealth is like losing weight. Everyone has a great plan, but few plans survive the collision with reality.

You can build wealth reliably by understanding the three principles of:

(1) Assets vs. liabilities
(2) Demographic changes
(3) Economic cycles

You also need a plan to put your hard-earned money into something that will put money into your pocket each month and not into something that will just eat a hole in your pocket. That is why it is critical to understand the difference between an "asset" and a "liability" and to put your hard-earned money into the assets.

Your private 401(k) savings are at risk. Like other countries, the U.S. will soon be forced to nationalize private 401(k) accounts and redistribute "excessively funded" accounts to bail out the underfunded union and municipal retirement programs.

If you retire with less than $12,000 saved, your 20-year retirement will be funded by somebody else. If you retire with more than $350,000 saved, *you* are that somebody else.

When you have climbed to the peak of the net worth mountain, take the time to look around; then enjoy strategically spending and gifting every remaining dollar you have earned.

Before they take it away and *before* you die... *spend it all.*

EPILOGUE
"Thank You for Working"

There was a time when I did not tip well because I believed that an overly generous reward system for the minimum wage workers would be a disincentive for them to make the extra effort to increase their education, skills training and ambitions. Why would they bother if they were already making enough money at their current job?

In 2013, while doing research for the "Redistribution" chapter, I became aware that in 30 states the government assistance programs (welfare) provide more value in benefits than one could earn by working full time at the minimum wage rate. So I asked myself, "In those 30 states why would anyone earning minimum wage bother to go to work when the government is incentivizing them to stay home?"

The answer is this: In America, almost without exception, people are motivated to improve themselves, improve their lives and get ahead. I believe that almost everyone; whether they were born in America, climbed a border fence or paddled a raft to our shores, has the pride, desire and motivation to better themselves. Granted, with some of us those attributes are obvious and with others we might have to look a little deeper. But I firmly believe that every American, if given the choice, would gladly trade all their government "free stuff" for a good paying job.

I now realize that by not tipping low wage earners I was only incentivizing them to say "The heck with this, I'd be better off qualifying for government assistance." So now I tip the waiter, the parking valet and the car wash attendants, with the hope that they will continue to work despite the fact the government is providing strong disincentives for them not to do so. When I get the telemarketer call during dinner, I am no longer rude, I am now polite, knowing that he or she is on *my* team because they are *working* for their money and they are doing a job I would not want to be doing.

Now when I tip, I make eye contact and I say "Thank you for working." I now realize, without exception, *every* worker is on *my* team.

And thus, I wage my one man "*Thank you for working*" campaign.

Please join.

Notes and References

Chapter One: Understanding Assets and Liabilities

CHAPTER ONE NOTES:

(1) Kiyosaki, Robert T., Sharon L. Lechter, *Rich Dad, Poor Dad*, Tech Press Inc., Paradise Valley, AZ, 1997, p. 52.

(2) Kiyosaki, Robert T., Cashflow Quadrant, Plata Publishing, Scottsdale, AZ, 2011, p. 241.

(3) Jones, Randall W., *The Richest Man in Town*, Hachette Book Group, New York, NY, 2009.

CHAPTER ONE REFERENCES:

Kiyosaki, Robert T., and Sharon L. Lechter, *Rich Dad, Poor Dad*, Tech Press Inc., Paradise Valley, AZ, 2007.

Kiyosaki, Robert T., and Sharon L. Lechter, *Rich Dad's Prophecy*, Warner Business Books, New York, NY, 2002.

Kiyosaki, Robert T., and Sharon L. Lechter, *Rich Dad's Cashflow Quadrant*, Plata Publishing, Scottsdale, AZ, 2011.

Kiyosaki, Robert T., and Sharon L. Lechter, *The Real Book of Real Estate*, Vanguard Press, New York, NY, 2009.

Smith, Keith Cameron, *The Top 10 Distinctions Between Millionaires and the Middle Class*, Random House, New York, NY, 2007.

Stanley, Thomas J., PhD., *The Millionaire Mind*, Andrews McMeel Publishing, Kansas City, MO, 2000.

Stanley, Thomas J., PhD., *The Millionaire Next Door*, Longstreet Press, Marietta, GA, 1996.

158 | BUILD WEALTH & *Spend It All*

Chapter Two: Understanding Economic Cycles

Chapter Two Notes:

(1) Burton, Theodore E., *Financial Crises and Periods of Industrial and Commercial Depression*, D. Appleton and Company, New York, NY, 1902 (2009), p. 65.

(2) Huerta de Soto, Jesus, *Money, Bank Credit and Economic Cycles*, Ludwig von Mises Institute, Auburn, AL, 1998.

(3) Shiller, Robert J., *Irrational Exuberance*, Princeton University Press, Princeton, NJ, 2005, p. 147.

(4) Prechter, Robert R., *Conquer The Crash*, 2002, John Wiley and Sons, Hoboken, NJ, p. 65

Chapter Two References:

Cecchetti, Stephen G., *Money, Banking and Financial Markets*, McGraw-Hill/Irwin, 2006.

Dent, Harry S., *The Great Boom Ahead*, Simon & Schuster, New York, NY, 1993.

Dent, Harry S. *The Great Crash Ahead*, Simon & Schuster, New York, NY, 2011.

Elias, David, *Dow 40,000*, McGraw-Hill Companies, New York, NY, 1999.

Glassman, James K., and Kevin A. Hassett, *Dow 36,000*, Random House, New York, NY, 1999.

Hoyt, Homer, *100 Years of Land of Values in Chicago: The Relationship of the Growth of Chicago to the Rise in Land Values 1830–1933*, University of Chicago Press, 1933.

Kadlec, Charles W., *Dow 100,000*, Prentice Hall Press, Paramus, NJ, 1999.

Kindleberger, Charles P., and Robert Z. Aliber, *Manias, Panics and Crashes*, Palgrave MacMillan, New York, NY, 2011.

Prechter, Robert R., *Conquer the Crash*, John Wiley and Sons, Hoboken, NJ, 2002.

Schiff, Peter, *Crash Proof,* John Wiley and Sons, Hoboken, NJ, 2007.
Schiff, Peter, *The Real Crash*, St. Martin's Press, New York, NY, 2012.
Schiller, Robert J., *International Exuberance*, Princeton University Press, Princeton, NJ, 2005.
www.Wikipedia.org/wiki/business_cycles
Zuccaro, Robert, *Dow 30,000 by 2008!: Why It's Different This Time*, Palisade Press, Jersey City, NJ, 2003.

Chapter Three: Understanding Demographics

CHAPTER THREE NOTES:

(1) Dent, Harry S., *The Next Great Bubble Boom*, Simon & Schuster, New York, NY, 2004, p. 145.
(2) Brooke, Christopher A., *Wealth Shift*, Penguin Group, New York, NY, 2006, p. 18.
(3) Brooke, Christopher A., *Wealth Shift*, Penguin Group, New York, NY, 2006, p. 25.
(4) Dent, Harry S., *The Great Boom Ahead*, Hyperion, New York, NY, 1993, p. 35.
(5) Dent, Harry S., *The Great Boom Ahead*, Hyperion, New York, NY, 1993, p. 35.
(6) Dent, Harry S., *The Roaring 2000s*, Simon & Schuster, New York, NY, 1998, p. 297.
(7) Brooke, Christopher A., *Wealth Shift*, Penguin Group, New York, NY, 2006, p. 47.
(8) Elmore, Tim, *Generation iY*, Poet Gardener Publishing, Atlanta, GA, 2010, p. 138.
(9) Elmore, Tim, *Generation iY*, Poet Gardener Publishing, Atlanta, GA, 2010, p. 172.
(10) Howe, Neil, and William Strauss, *Millennials Rising*, Random House, New York, NY, 2000, p. 318.
(11) Brooke, Christopher A., *Wealth Shift*, Penguin Group, New York, NY, 2006, p. 25.

(12) Brooke, Christopher A., *Wealth Shift*, Penguin Group, New York, NY, 2006, p. 30.

(13) Brooke, Christopher A., *Wealth Shift*, Penguin Group, New York, NY, 2006, p. 30.

(14) Brooke, Christopher A., *Wealth Shift*, Penguin Group, New York, NY, 2006, p. 30.

(15) Arnold, Daniel A., *The Great Bust Ahead*, Vorago-US, 2002, p. 17.

(16) Arnold, Daniel A., *The Great Bust Ahead*, 2002, Vorago-US, p. 52.

(17) Strauss, William and Neil Howe, *The Fourth Turning*, Bantam Doubleday Dell Publishing Group, New York, NY, 1997, p. 315.

(18) Dent, Harry S., *The Next Great Bubble Boom*, Hyperion, New York, NY, 2004, p. 89.

(19) Strauss, William, and Neil Howe, *Generations*, William Morrow and Co., New York, NY, 1991, p. 382.

CHAPTER THREE REFERENCES:

Alsop, Ron, *The Trophy Kids Grow Up*, Jossey-Bass, San Francisco, CA, 2008.

Anderson, Clifford, *The Stages of Life*, Atlantic Monthly Press, New York, NY, 1995.

Dent, Harry S., *The Great Depression Ahead*, Simon & Schuster, New York, NY, 2008.

Dent, Harry S., *The Great Crash Ahead*, Simon & Schuster, New York, NY, 2011.

Dent, Harry S., *The Demographic Cliff*, Penguin Group, New York, NY, 2014.

Howe, Neil, and William Strauss, *Millennial Rising*, Random House, New York, NY, 2000.

Kotlikoff, Laurence J., and Scott Burns, *The Coming Generational Storm*, MIT Press, Cambridge, MA, 2005.

WSJ "Opinion", "The Entitlement Panic," *Wall Street Journal*, 2006.

Chapter Four: Redistribution and Your Wealth

Chapter Four Notes:

(1) Hayek, F.A., *The Constitution of Liberty*, University of Chicago Press, Chicago, IL, 1960 (reprinted 2011), p. 133.

(2) Marx, Karl, *The Communist Manifesto*, International Publishers, New York, NY, 1848 (reprinted 2014).

(3) De Tocqueville, Alex, *Democracy in America*, (1835) Welch, Bigelow and Company, Cambridge, UK, reprinted by Penguin Classics, New York, NY, 2003.

(4) Friedman, Milton, and Rose F. Friedman, *Free To Choose*, Harcourt Inc., Orlando, FL, 1980.

(5) Walsh, Matt, "How Did This Happen? A Cosmic Collision," *Business Observer*, 2013.

(6) Aguiar, Mark, and Erik Hurst, "Measuring Trends in Leisure: The Allocation of Time Over Five Decades," *The Quarterly Journal of Economics*, Vol. 122, issue 3, pp. 969–1006.

(7) WSJ "Opinion", "Their Fair Share," *Wall Street Journal*, 2008.

(8) WSJ "Opinion", "How Much the Rich Pay," *Wall Street Journal*, 2012.

(9) Laing, Jonathan R., "Slowing to a Crawl," *Barron's*, 2013.

(10) Theobald, Robert, *The Rapids of Change*, Knowledge Systems, Indianapolis, IN, 1987.

(11) Young, Fred J., *How To Get Rich and Stay Rich*, Lifetime Periodicals, Hollywood, FL, 1996, p. 128.

(12) Sowell, Thomas, *Economic Facts and Fallacies*, Basic Books, New York, NY, 2007, p. 128.

(13) Gilder, George, *Wealth and Poverty*, Regney Publishing Inc., Washington, D.C., 2012, p. 103.

(14) Jefferson, Thomas, and John Kaminski, *Quotable Jefferson*, Princeton University Press, Princeton, NJ, 2006, p. 31.

(15) Bovard, James, *Attention Deficit Democracy*, Palgrave Macmillan, New York, NY, 2006, p. 129.

(16) Friedman, Milton, *Capitalism and Freedom*, University of Chicago Press, Chicago, IL, 1962, p. 174.

(17) Griffin, G. Edward, *The Creature From Jekyll Island*, American Media, Westlake Village, CA, 1994, p. 509.

(18) Menchen, H. L., *Notes on Democracy*, Alfred A. Knopf, New York, NY, 1926, reprinted CreateSpace Independent Publishing, 2013.

(19) Pento, Michael, *The Coming Bond Market Collapse*, John Wiley & Sons, Hoboken, NJ, 2013, p. 282.

(20) Worsley, F. A., *Endurance*, W.W. Norton and Co., Inc., New York, NY, 1931.

CHAPTER FOUR REFERENCES:

Aguiar, Mark, and Erik Hurst, "Measuring Trends in Leisure: The Allocation of Time Over Five Decades," *The Quarterly Journal of Economics*, Vol. 122, issue 3, pp. 969–1006.

Bialik, Carl, "Hurdles for New Line on Poverty," *Wall Street Journal*, 2013.

Bonner, Bill, and Addison Wiggin, *Empire of Debt*, John Wiley & Sons, Inc., Hoboken, NJ, 2006.

Bovard, James, *Attention Deficit Democracy*, Palgrave Macmillan, New York, NY, 2007.

Cowen, Tyler, *Average is Over*, Penguin Books, New York, NY, 2013.

Eberstadt, Nicholas, *A Nation of Takers*, Templeton Press, PA, 2012.

Ferguson, Niall, *The Great Degeneration*, Penguin Press, New York, NY, 2012.

Friedman, Milton, *Capitalism and Freedom*, University of Chicago Press, Chicago, IL, 1962.

Friedman, Milton, and Rose F. Friedman, *Free To Choose*, University of Chicago Press, Chicago, IL, 1980.

Furchtgott-Roth, Diana, "The Truth About Income Inequality," *Wall Street Journal*, 2013.

Gilder, George, *Wealth and Poverty*, Regnery Publishing Inc., Washington, D.C., 1981.

Gladwell, Malcolm, *The Tipping Point*, Little, Brown and Company, Boston, MA, 2010.

Griffin, G. Edward, *The Creature From Jekyll Island*, American Media, Westlake Village, CA, 1994 (reprinted 2009).

Hayek, F.A., *Constitution of Liberty*, University of Chicago Press, Chicago, IL, 1960 (reprinted 2011).

Hayek, F.A., *The Road To Serfdom*, University of Chicago Press, Chicago, IL, 1944 (reprinted 2007).

Herrnstein, Richard J., and Charles Murray, *The Bell Curve*, Simon & Schuster, New York, NY, 1994.

Hill, Napoleon, *Think and Grow Rich*, Fawcett Books, NY, 1960.

Kaletsky, Anatole, *Capitalism 4.0*, Perseus Books Group, Philadelphia, PA, 2010.

Laffer, Arthur B., and Stephen Moore, *The End of Prosperity*, Simon & Schuster, New York, NY, 2008.

Lansing, Alfred, *Endurance*, Perseus Books Group, Philadelphia, PA, 1959.

McLeod, S. S., *Edward Thorndike*, Retrieved from http://www.simplypsychology.org, 2007.

Menchen, H. L., *Notes on Democracy*, Alfred A. Knopf, New York, NY, 1926, reprinted CreateSpace Independent Publishing, 2013.

Murray, Charles, *Coming Apart*, Crown Publishing Group, New York, NY, 2012.

Perkins, Dennis N.T., *Leading at the Edge*, American Management Association, New York, NY, 2000.

Pento, Michael, *The Coming Bond Market Collapse*, John Wiley & Sons, Hoboken, NJ, 2013.

Rector, Robert, "How the War on Poverty Was Lost," *Wall Street Journal*, 2014.

Reynolds, Alan, *Income and Wealth*, Greenwood Press, Westport, CT, 2006.

Smith, Adam, *The Wealth of Nations*, Thrifty Books, Blacksburg, VA, 1776 (reprinted 2009).

Sowell, Thomas, *Economic Facts and Fallacies*, Basic Books, New York, NY, 2007.

Stanley, Thomas J., PhD., and William D. Danko, PhD., *The Millionaire Next Door*, Longstreet Press, Atlanta, GA, 1996.

Stanley, Thomas J., PhD., *The Millionaire Mind*, Andrews McMeel Publishing, Kansas City, MO, 2000.

Tanner, Michael D., and Charles Hughes, "The Work Versus Welfare Trade-Off: 2013," Cato Institute White Paper, 2013.

Tergesen, Anne, "How to Maximize Your Social Security Benefits," *Wall Street Journal*, 2013.

"A Memo to Obama," *The Economist*, 2014.

Chapter Five: 401(k): They're Coming to Take It Away

CHAPTER FIVE NOTES:

(1) Stein, Ben, and Phil DeMuth, *The Little Book of Bulletproof Investing*, John Wiley & Sons, Inc., Hoboken, NJ, 2010, p. 101.

(2) Ghilarducci, Teresa, "Why the 401(k) is a Failed Experiment," 2013, http://wwwpbs.org.

(3) Pento, Michael, *The Coming Bond Market Collapse*, John Wiley & Sons, Inc., Hoboken, 2013, p. 228.

(4) Brooke, Christopher A., *Wealth Shift*, Penguin Books, New York, NY, 2006, p. 31.

CHAPTER FIVE REFERENCES:

Bogle, John C., *Enough*, John Wiley & Sons, Inc., Hoboken, NJ, 2009.

Bogle, John C., *The Little Book of Common Sense Investing*, John Wiley & Sons, Inc., Hoboken, NJ, 2007.

Brooke, Christopher A., *Wealth Shift*, Penguin Books, New York, NY, 2006.

Callahan, David, *A Perfect Failure: Why the 401(k) Has Been a Flop*, http://www.huffingtonpost.com/david-callahan/401k-a-perfect-failure_b_1574834.html, 2012.

Ghilarducci, Teresa, "Guaranteed Retirement Accounts, Toward Retirement Income Security," EPI Briefing Paper #204, Economic Policy Institute, 2007.

Ghilarducci, Teresa, "The Plot Against Pensions and the Plan to Save Them," http://www.youtube.com/watch?v=hGNBW0agjWU, 2009.

Ghilarducci, Teresa, *When I'm Sixty-Four, The Plot against Pensions and the Plan to Save Them*, Princeton University Press, Princeton, NJ, 2008.

Ghilarducci, Teresa, "Why the 401(k) is a Failed Experiment," http://www .pbs.org/wgbh/pages/frontline/business-economy-financial-crisis/retirement-gamble/teresa-ghilarducci-why-the-401k-is-a-failed-experiment/, 2013.

Malkiel, Burton, G., *A Random Walk Down Wall Street*, W.W. Norton & Co., New York, NY, 1973 (reprinted 2012).

"National Senior Council Battles Government Efforts to Seize Private Retirement Savings," http://www.nationalseniorcouncil.org, 2014.

"Pension Funds Assess Investments in Government Debt," *Financial Times*, http://wwwft.com, 2012.

Pento, Michael, *The Coming Bond Market Collapse*, John Wiley & Sons, Inc., Hoboken, NJ, 2013.

Siegel, Jeremy J., *Stocks For The Long Run*, McGraw-Hill, New York, NY, 2014.

"The 401(k) Confiscation: The Ghilarducci Plan," http://www.nc renegade.com/editorial/the-401k-confiscation-the-ghilarducci-plan-ann-barnhardt/, 2012.

"The Plan to Steal Your 401(k)," http://www.rushlimbaugh.com/daily/2012/11/29/details_the_plan_to_steal_your_401_k, 2012.

Time magazine cover, 2009.

"Will Obama Really Confiscate Your Retirement Savings?," http://www .fool.com/retirement/general/2013/04/21/will-obama-really-confiscate-your-retirement-savin.aspx, 2013.

Chapter Six: The Coming U.S. Default

CHAPTER SIX NOTES:

(1) Barrett, Tom, "US Has Already Defaulted on its Debt – Several Times," http://www.conservativetruth.org/article.php?id=3738, 2013.

(2) Keynes, John Maynard, "The Economic Consequences of the Peace," Macmillan, London, 1919, reprinted by CreateSpace Independent Publishing 2012.

(3) Krugman, Paul, *End This Depression Now*, W.W. Norton & Company, Inc., New York, NY, 2013, p. 165.

(4) Gross, Bill, "Investing Outlook," *PIMCO newsletter*, April 2011.

(5) Bonner, Bill, and Addison Wiggin, *Empire of Debt*, John Wiley & Sons, Hoboken, NJ, 2006, p. 249.

(6) Meeker, Mary, "USA Inc.," KPCB.com, 2011, p. 210.

(7) Krugman, Paul, *End This Depression Now*, W.W. Norton & Company, New York, NY, 2013, p. 183.

(8) Krugman, Paul, *End This Depression Now*, W.W. Norton & Company, New York, NY, 2013, p. 183.

(9) Krugman, Paul, *End This Depression Now*, W.W. Norton & Company, New York, NY, 2013, p. 141.

(10) Bonner, Bill, and Addison Wiggin, *Empire of Debt*, John Wiley & Sons, Hoboken, NJ, 2006, p. 249.

(11) Schiff, Peter, *The Real Crash*, St. Martin's Press, New York, NY, 2012, p. 270.

CHAPTER SIX REFERENCES:

247Alex, "Thirteen American Cities Going Broke," http://www.247wallst.com, 10/25/12.

Bonner, Bill, and Addison Wiggin, *Empire of Debt*, John Wiley & Sons, Hoboken, NJ, 2006.

Borensztein, Edwardo, and Ugo Panizza, "The Cost of Sovereign Default," *IMF Working Paper*, wp/08/238, October 2008.

Cass, Connie, "U.S. Never Defaulted on Debt? Not So Fast," http://www.huffingtonpost.com, 2013.

Chamberlain, John S., "A Short History of U.S. Credit Defaults," http://www.mises.org, 2011.

Farmer, Liz, "Bondholders Losing Ground in City Bankruptcies," http://www.governing.com. 2013.

Ferguson, Niall, *Colossus: The Rise and Fall of the American Empire*, Penguin Books, New York, NY, 2005.

Glover, John, "U.S. May Join Germany of 1933 in Pantheon of Defaults," http://www.bloomberg.com, 2013.

Griffin, G. Edward, *The Creature of Jekyll Island*, American Media, Westlake Village, CA, 1994 (reprinted 2009).

Kotlikoff, Laurence J. and Scott Burns, *The Clash of Generations: Saving Ourselves, Our Kids and Our Economy*, MIT Press, Cambridge, MA, 2012.

Krugman, Paul, *End This Depression Now*, W.W. Norton & Company, Inc., New York, NY, 2013.

Maciag, Mike, "How Rare Are Municipal Bankruptcies?," http://www.governing.com, 2013.

Meeker, Mary, "USA Inc.," KPCB.com, 2011.

Pento, Michael, *The Coming Bond Market Collapse*, John Wiley & Sons, Inc., Hoboken, NJ, 2013.

Polloch, Alex J., "Was There Ever a Default on U.S. Treasury Debt?," http://www.americanspectator.com, 2009.

Reinhart, Carmen, and Kenneth Rogoff, "The Forgotten History of Domestic Debt," National Bureau of Economic Research, 2008.

Reinhart, Carmen, and Kenneth Rogoff, *This Time Is Different*, Princeton University Press, Princeton, NJ, 2009.

Schiff, Peter, *The Real Crash*, St. Martin's Press, New York, NY, 2012.

Steil, Benn, *The Battle of Bretton Woods*, Princeton University Press, Princeton, NJ, 2013.

Steiner, Sheyna, "How to Avoid Municipal Bonds That Default," http://www.bankrate.com. 2013.

Washingtons Blog, "The Myth That U.S. Has Never Defaulted On Its Debt," http://www.ritholtz.com/blog/2013/10/the-myth-that-u-s-has-never-defaulted-on-its-debt/, 2013.

Zweig, Jason, "Our Government Bonds? Here's Why You Should Be Worried," http://www.online.wsj.com, 2011.

Chapter Seven: Lifestyle: You Have Choices

CHAPTER SEVEN NOTES:

(1) Robin, Vicki, and Joe Dominguez, *Your Money or Your Life*, Penguin Press, New York, NY, 1992 (reprinted 2008), p. 52.

(2) Robin, Vicki, and Joe Dominguez, *Your Money or Your Life*, Penguin Press, New York, NY, 1992 (reprinted 2008), p. 23.

(3) Robin, Vicki, and Joe Dominguez, *Your Money or Your Life*, Penguin Press, New York, NY, 1992 (reprinted 2008), p. 243.

CHAPTER SEVEN REFERENCES:

Herskovitis, Melville J., *Economic Anthropology*, Norton, New York, NY, 1965.

Lee, Richard, "Kung Bushman Subsistence: An Input-Output Analysis," in A. Vayda (ed.) *Environment and Cultural Behavior*, Natural History Press, Garden City, NY, 1969.

Mountford, C. P., (ed.) "1960 Records of the 1948 American-Australian Scientific Expedition to Arnhem Land, Vol. 2," *Anthropology and Nutrition*, Melbourne University Press, 1960.

Stahlins, Marshall, *Stone Age Economics*, Walter de Gruyter, Inc., Hawthorne, NY, 1974.

Woodburn, James, "An Introduction to Hadza Ecology," in R. Lee and I. DeVore (eds), *Man And The Hunter*, Aldine Press, Chicago, 2009.

Chapter Eight: Enjoy Your Wealth and Spend It All

CHAPTER EIGHT NOTES:

(1) Pollan, Stephen M., and Mark Levine, "Die Broke," *Worth* magazine, July/August 1995.

(2) Pollan, Stephen M., and Mark Levine, *Die Broke*, Harper Business, New York, NY, 1997 (reprinted 2005).

(3) Dent, Harry S., *The Great Crash Ahead*, Free Press, New York, NY, 2011, p. 35.

(4) Bogle, John, C., *Enough*, John Wiley & Sons, Hoboken, NJ, 2009, p. 47.

(5) Bogle, John, C., *The Little Book of Common Sense Investing*, John Wiley & Sons, Hoboken, NJ, 2007, p. xv.

(6) Bogle, John, C., *Enough*, John Wiley & Sons, Hoboken, NJ, 2009, p. 35.

(7) Bogle, John, C., *The Little Book of Common Sense Investing*, John Wiley & Sons, Inc., Hoboken, NJ, 2007, p. xxiii.

(8) Malkiel, Burton G., *A Random Walk Down Wall Street*, W.W. Norton & Co., New York, NY, 1973 (reprinted 2012), p. 17.

(9) Malkiel, Burton G., *A Random Walk Down Wall Street*, W.W. Norton & Co., New York, NY, 1973 (reprinted 2012), p. 17.

(10) Malkiel, Burton G., *A Random Walk Down Wall Street*, John Wiley & Sons, Hoboken, NJ, 1973 (reprinted 2012).

(11) Arnott, Robert D., Jason Hsu, Vitali Kalesnik, and Phil Tyndall, "The Surprising Alpha from Malkiel's Monkey and Upside-Down Strategies," in *The Journal of Portfolio Management*, Summer 2013, Vol. 39, No. 4: pp. 91–105.

(12) Kate4Kim, Partners4Prosperity.com/three-monkeys-and-a-cat-picking-stocks, 2013.

Chapter Eight References:

Arnott, Robert D., Jason Hsu, Vitali Kalesnik, and Phil Tyndall, "The Surprising Alpha from Malkiel's Monkey and Upside-Down Strategies," in *The Journal of Portfolio Management*, Summer 2013, Vol. 39, No. 4: pp. 91–105.

Baldwin, William, "The Case for Dying Broke," *Forbes*, 2012.

Bogle, John C., *Enough*, John Wiley & Sons, Hoboken, NJ, 2009.

Bogle, John C., *The Little Book of Common Sense Investing*, John Wiley & Sons, Hoboken, NJ, 2007.

Bodie, Zivi, and Rachaelle Taqqu, *Risk Less and Prosper More*, John Wiley & Sons, Hoboken, NJ, 2012.

Dent, Harry S., *The Great Crash Ahead*, Free Press, New York, NY, 2011.

Kotlikoff, Laurence J., and Scott Burns, *The Coming Generational Storm*, MIT Press, Cambridge, MA, 2005.

Kotlikoff, Laurence J., *Spend Til the End*, Simon & Schuster, New York, NY, 2008.

Larimore, Taylor, Mel Lindauer, Richard A. Ferri, and Laura F. Dogu, *The Boglehead's Guide to Retirement Planning*, John Wiley & Sons, Hoboken, NJ, 2009.

Malkiel, Burton G., *A Random Walk Down Wall Street*, John Wiley & Sons, Hoboken, NJ, 1973 (reprinted 2012).

Malkiel, Burton G., *A Random Walk Guide to Investing: Ten Rules for Financial Success*, John Wiley & Sons, Hoboken, NJ, 2003.

Partners4Prosperity.com/three-monkeys-and-a-cat-picking-stocks, 2013.

Pollan, Stephen M., and Mark Levine, *Die Broke*, Harper Business, New York, NY, 1997 (reprinted 2005).

Pollan, Stephen M., and Mark Levine, "Die Broke," *Worth Magazine*, July/August 1995.

Pollan, Stephen M. and Mark Levine, *Live Rich and Die Broke*, HarperCollins, New York, NY, 2005.

Shilling, Gary A., *The Age of Deleveraging*, John Wiley & Sons, Hoboken, NJ, 2011.

Siegel, Jeremy, J., *The Future For Investors*, Crown Business, New York, NY, 2005.

Siegel, Jeremy, J., *Stocks For the Long Run*, McGraw-Hill, New York, NY, 1994 (reprinted 2014).

Stein, Ben, and Phil DeMuth, *The Little Book of Bulletproof Investing*, John Wiley & Sons, Inc, Hoboken, NJ, 2010.

Zitz, Michael, *Giving It All Away: The Doris Buffett Story*, The Permanent Press, Sag Harbor, NY, 2010.

401(k) Plan Fee Menu

FEES THAT CAN BE CHARGED TO YOUR RETIREMENT ACCOUNT BY YOUR 401(K) ADMINISTRATOR. (Taken from a 401(k) administrator report for the industry.)

(1) Investment management	(14) Brokerage
(2) Bookkeeping	(15) Valuation
(3) Administrative fees	(16) TPA fees
(4) Accounting	(17) Custodial/document
(5) Auditing	(18) Purchase fees
(6) Actuarial services	(19) Expense ratio
(7) Appraisal	(20) Expense fees
(8) Banking	(21) IRA rollover
(9) Consulting	(22) Fund co. fees
(10) Investment management	(23) Loan maintenance
(11) Insurance	(24) Origination fee
(12) Advisory	(25) Distribution
(13) Legal	(26) Withdrawal fee

Actuarial Table

Actuarial Life Table

Age	Years Left (Male)	Years Left (Female)	Age	Years Left (Male)	Years Left (Female)
0	75.9	80.8	20	56.8	61.5
1	75.4	80.3	21	55.9	60.6
2	74.5	79.3	22	55.0	59.6
3	73.5	78.3	23	54.0	58.6
4	72.5	77.3	24	53.1	57.6
5	71.5	76.3	25	52.2	56.7
6	70.5	75.4	26	51.2	55.7
7	69.5	74.4	27	50.3	54.7
8	68.5	73.4	28	49.4	53.8
9	67.5	72.4	29	48.4	52.8
10	66.6	71.4	30	47.5	51.8
11	65.6	70.4	31	46.6	50.9
12	64.6	69.4	32	45.6	49.9
13	63.6	68.4	33	44.7	48.9
14	62.6	67.4	34	43.8	48.0
15	61.6	66.4	35	42.9	47.0
16	60.6	65.5	36	42.0	46.0
17	59.7	64.5	37	41.0	45.1
18	58.7	63.5	38	40.1	44.1
19	57.8	62.5	39	39.1	43.2

Age	Years Left (Male)	Years Left (Female)	Age	Years Left (Male)	Years Left (Female)
40	38.2	42.2	72	12.7	14.9
41	37.3	41.3	73	12.1	14.2
42	36.4	40.3	74	11.5	13.5
43	35.5	39.4	75	10.9	12.8
44	34.6	38.5	76	10.2	12.1
45	33.5	37.5	77	9.7	11.5
46	32.8	36.6	78	9.2	10.9
47	32.0	35.7	79	8.6	10.2
48	31.1	34.8	80	8.1	9.6
49	30.2	33.9	81	7.6	9.1
50	29.3	33.0	82	7.1	8.5
51	28.5	32.1	83	6.7	8.0
52	27.7	31.2	84	6.2	7.4
53	26.8	30.4	85	5.8	7.0
54	26.0	29.5	86	5.4	6.5
55	25.2	28.6	87	5.0	6.0
56	24.4	27.7	88	4.7	5.6
57	23.6	26.9	89	4.3	5.2
58	22.8	26.0	90	4.0	4.8
59	22.0	25.1	91	3.7	4.5
60	21.3	24.3	92	3.5	4.2
61	20.5	23.5	93	3.2	3.9
62	19.7	22.6	94	3.0	3.6
63	19.0	21.8	95	2.8	3.4
64	18.2	21.0	96	2.6	3.2
65	17.5	20.2	97	2.5	3.0
66	16.8	19.4	98	2.4	2.8
67	16.1	18.6	99	2.2	2.6
68	15.4	17.8	100	2.1	2.5
69	14.7	17.1	105	1.6	1.8
70	14.0	16.3	110	2.0	1.3
71	13.5	15.5	115	0.8	0.9

http://www.ssa.gov/OACT/STATS/

Famous Bubbles in History

Item	percent increase	percent decrease
Tulips Holland (1634–1637)	+5,900 percent	−93 percent
Miss. Shares France (1719–1721)	+6,200 percent	−99 percent
South Seas shares Great Britain (1719–1720)	+1,000 percent	−84 percent
U. S. stocks United States (1921–1932)	+497 percent	−87 percent
Mexican stocks Mexico (1978–1981)	+785 percent	−73 percent
Silver United States (1979–1982)	+710 percent	−88 percent

Hong Kong stocks
Hong Kong
(1970–1974)   +1,200 percent   −92 percent

Taiwan stocks
Taiwan
(1986–1990)   +40 percent   −80 percent

NASDAQ tech stocks
United States
(1999–2000)   +60 percent   −78 percent

Cecchetti (2006)

Also:
Housing Boom
United States
(2000–2009)   +100 percent   −35 percent

Bibliography

(Bold = must read)

Alsop, Ron, *The Trophy Kids Grow Up*, Jossey-Bass, San Francisco, CA, 2008.

Arnold, David A., *The Great Bust Ahead*, Vorago-US, 2002.

Arnott, Robert D., Jason Hsu, Vitali Kalesnik, and Phil Tyndall, "The Surprising Alpha From Malkiel's Monkey and Upside-Down Strategies," in *The Journal of Portfolio Management*, Summer 2013, Vol. 39, No. 4: pp. 91–105.

Baldwin, William, "The Case For Dying Broke," *Forbes*, 2012.

Barrett, Tom, "The U.S. Has Already Defaulted On Its Debt – Several Times," http://www.conservativetruth.org, 2013.

Bernanke, Ben S. *The Federal Reserve and the Financial Crisis*, Princeton University Press, Princeton, NJ, 2013.

Bodie, Zivi, and Rachaelle Taqqu, *Risk Less and Prosper More*, John Wiley & Sons, Hoboken, NJ, 2012.

Bogle, John, C., *Enough*, John Wiley & Sons, Hoboken, NJ, 2009.

Bogle, John, C., *The Little Book of Common Sense Investing*, John Wiley & Sons, Hoboken, NJ, 2007.

Bonner, Bill, and Addison Wiggin, *Empire of Debt*, John Wiley & Sons, Hoboken, NJ, 2006.

Brooke, Christopher A., *Wealth Shift*, Penguin Group, New York, NY, 2006.

Bovard, James, *Attention Deficit Democracy*, Palgrave Macmillan, New York, NY, 2007.

Burton, Theodore E., *Financial Crises*, D. Appleton and Company, New York, NY, 1902 (2008).

Business Cycles. www.Wikipedia.org/wiki/business_cycles

Callahan, David, *A Perfect Failure: Why the 401(k) Has Been a Flop*, http://www.Huffingtonpost.com, 2013.

Cass, Connie, "U.S. Never Defaulted on Debt? Not So Fast," http://www.huffingtonpost.com, 2013.

Cecchetti, Stephen G., *Money, Banking and Financial Markets*, McGraw-Hill/Irwin, New York, NY, 2006.

Chamberlain, John S., "A Short History of U.S. Credit Defaults," http://www.mises.org, 2011.

http://www.coinflation.com

Cowen, Tyler, *Average is Over*, Penguin Books, New York, NY, 2013.

Dent, Harry S., *The Demographic Cliff*, Penguin Group, New York, NY, 2014.

Dent, Harry S., *The Great Crash Ahead*, Free Press, New York, NY, 2011. Simon & Schuster, New York, NY, 2008.

Dent, Harry S., *The Next Great Bubble Boom*, Simon & Schuster, New York, NY, 2004.

Dent, Harry S., *The Roaring 2000s*, Simon & Schuster, New York, NY, 1998.

Eberstadt, Nicholas, *A Nation of Takers*, Templeton Press, West Conshohocken, PA, 2012.

Elmore, Tim, *Generation iY*, Poet Gardener Publishing, Atlanta, GA, 2010.

Elwell, Craig K., *Brief History of the Gold Standard in the United States*, Congressional Research Service, 2011.

Ferguson, Niall, *Colossus: The Rise and Fall of the American Empire*, Penguin Books, New York, NY, 2005.

Ferguson, Niall, *The Great Degeneration*, Penguin Press, New York, NY, 2012.

Fisher, Irving, *Booms & Depressions*, (Adelphi Company, New York, 1932), reprinted ThaiSunset Publications, Thailand, 2009.

Friedman, Milton, *Capitalism and Freedom*, University of Chicago Press, Chicago, IL, 1962 (reprinted 2002).

Friedman, Milton, and Rose F. Friedman, *Free To Choose*, Harcourt Inc., Orlando, FL, 1980.

Ghilarducci, Teresa, *When I'm Sixty-Four, The Plot against Pensions and the Plan to Save Them*, Princeton University Press, Princeton, NJ, 2008.

Gilder, George, *Wealth and Poverty*, Regnery Publishing Inc., Washington, D.C., 2012.

Glassman, James K., and Kevin A. Hassett, *Dow 36,000*, Random House Inc., New York, NY, 1999.

Glover, John, *U.S. May Join Germany of 1933 in Pantheon of Defaults*, http://www.bloomberg.com, 2013.

Griffin, G. Edward, *The Creature From Jekyll Island*, American Media, Westlake Village, CA, 1994.

Hayek, F.A., *The Constitution of Liberty*, University of Chicago Press, Chicago, IL, 1960 (reprinted 2011).

Hayek, F.A., *The Road to Serfdom*, University of Chicago Press, Chicago, IL, 1944 (reprinted 2007).

Herrnstein, Richard J., and Charles Murray, *The Bell Curve*, Simon & Schuster, New York, NY, 1994.

Hewitt, Mike, "The Fate of Paper Money," http://www.DollarDaze.org, 2009.

Hill, Napoleon, *Think and Grow Rich*, Fawcett Books, NY, 1960.

Howe, Neil, and William Strauss, *Millennials Rising*, Random House, New York, NY, 2000.

Hubbard, Glen and Tim Kane, *Balance*, Simon & Schuster, New York, NY, 2013.

Jones, Randall W., *The Richest Man in Town*, Hachette Book Group, New York, NY, 2009.

Kate4Kim, "Three Monkeys and a Cat Picking Stocks," http://www.Partners4Prosperity.com. 1/24/2013.

Keynes, John Maynard, *The General Theory of Employment, Interest and Money*, Harcourt, Brace and Company, New York, NY, (1935), reprinted Classic Books America, New York, NY, 2009.

Kindleberger, Charles P., and Robert Z. Aliber, *Manias, Panics and Crashes*, 2011.

Kiyosaki, Robert T., and Sharon L. Lechter, *The Real Book of Real Estate*, Vanguard Press, New York, NY, 2009.

Kiyosaki, Robert T., and Sharon L. Lechter, *Rich Dad's Cashflow Quadrant*, Plata Publishing, Scottsdale, AZ, 2011.

Kiyosaki, Robert T., and Sharon L. Lechter, *Rich Dad's Conspiracy of the Rich*, Hachette Book Group, New York, NY, 2009.

Kiyosaki, Robert T., Sharon L. Lechter, *Rich Dad, Poor Dad*, Tech Press Inc., Paradise Valley, AZ, 2011.

Kiyosaki, Robert T., and Sharon L. Lechter, *Rich Dad's Prophecy*, Warner Business Books, New York, NY, 2013.

Kotlikoff, Laurence J., *Spend Til the End*, Simon & Schuster, New York, NY, 2008.

Kotlikoff, Laurence J., and Scott Burns, *The Clash of Generations: Saving Ourselves, Our Kids and Our Economy*, MIT Press, Cambridge, MA, 2012.

Kotlikoff, Laurence J., and Scott Burns, *The Coming Generational Storm*, MIT Press, Cambridge, MA, 2005.

Krugman, Paul, *End This Depression Now*, W.W. Norton & Company, New York, NY, 2013.

Laffer, Arthur B., and Stephen Moore, *Return to Prosperity*, Simon & Schuster, New York, NY, 2010.

Laffer, Arthur B., and Stephen Moore, *The End of Prosperity*, Simon & Schuster, New York, NY, 2008.

Lansing, Alfred, *Endurance*, (Caroll & Graf, 1986) Perseus Books Group, Philadelphia, PA, 1999.

Larimore, Taylor, Mel Lindauer, Richard A. Ferri, and Laura F. Dogu, *The Boglehead's Guide to Retirement Planning*, John Wiley & Sons, Inc., Hoboken, NJ, 2009.

Malkiel, Burton G., *A Random Walk Down Wall Street*, W.W. Norton & Co., New York, NY, 1973 (reprinted 2012).

Meeker, Mary, "USA Inc.," KPCB.com, 2011.

Minsky, Hyman P., *John Maynard Keynes*, (Columbia University Press, 1975), McGraw-Hill, New York, NY, 2008.

Mises, Ludwig von, *The Theory of Money and Credit*, (Germany, 1952), Signalman Publishing, Orlando, FL, 2009.

Murray, Charles, *Coming Apart*, Crown Publishing Group, New York, NY, 2012.

Pento, Michael, *The Coming Bond Market Collapse*, John Wiley & Sons, Hoboken, NJ, 2013.

Pollan, Stephen M., and Mark Levine, *Die Broke*, Harper Business, New York, NY, 1997 (reprinted 2005).

Pollan, Stephen M., and Mark Levine, *Live Rich, Die Broke*, HarperCollins Publishing, New York, NY, 2005).

Polloch, Alex J., "Was There Ever a Default on US Treasury Debt?" http://www.americanspectator.com, 2009.

Prechter, Robert R., *Conquer the Crash*, John Wiley and Sons, Inc., Hoboken, NJ, 2002.

Reinhart, Carmen, and Kenneth Rogoff, *The Forgotten History of Domestic Debt*, National Bureau of Economic Research, 2008.

Reinhart, Carmen, and Kenneth Rogoff, *This Time Is Different*, Princeton University Press, Princeton, NJ, 2009.

Robin, Vicki and Joe Dominguez, *Your Money or Your Life*, Penguin Press, New York, NY, 1992 (reprinted 2008).

Schiff, Peter, *Crash Proof*, John Wiley and Sons, Hoboken, NJ, 2007.

Schiff, Peter, *The Real Crash*, St. Martin's Press, New York, NY 2012.

Schumpeter, Joseph, A., *Capitalism, Socialism and Democracy*, Harper & Row, New York, NY, 1942.

Shiller, Robert J., *Irrational Exuberance*, Princeton University Press, Princeton, NJ, 2005.

Shilling, Gary A., *The Age of Deleveraging*, John Wiley & Sons, Inc, Hoboken, NJ, 2011.

Siegel, Jeremy J., *Stocks For The Long Run*, McGraw-Hill, New York, NY, 2014.

Siegel, Jeremy, J., *The Future for Investors*, Crown Business, New York, NY, 2005.

Smith, Adam, *The Wealth of Nations*, Thrifty Books, Blacksburg, VA, 1776/2009.

Smith, Keith Cameron, *The Top 10 Distinctions Between Millionaires and the Middle Class*, Random House, New York, NY, 2007.

Sowell, Thomas, *Economic Facts and Fallacies*, Basic Books, New York, NY, 2007.

Stahlins, Marshall, *Stone Age Economics*, Walter de Gruyter, Hawthorne, NY, 1974.

Stanley, Thomas J., PhD., *The Millionaire Mind*, Andrews McMeel Publishing, Kansas City, MO, 2000.

Stanley, Thomas J., PhD., *The Millionaire Next Door*, Longstreet Press, Inc., Marietta, GA, 1996.

Steil, Benn, and Manuel Hinds, *Money, Markets and Sovereignty*, Yale University Press, New Haven, CT, 2010.

Steil, Benn, *The Battle of Bretton Woods*, Princeton University Press, Princeton, NJ, 2013.

Stein, Ben, and Phil DeMuth, *The Little Book of Bulletproof Investing*, John Wiley & Sons, Inc, Hoboken, NJ, 2010.

Steiner, Sheyna, "How to Avoid Municipal Bonds That Default," http://www.bankrate.com. 2013.

Strauss, William, and Neil Howe, *Generations*, William Morrow and Co., New York, NY, 1991.

Strauss, William, and Neil Howe, *The Fourth Turning*, Bantam Doubleday Dell Publishing Group, New York, NY, 1997.

Theobald, Robert, *The Rapids of Change*, Knowledge Systems, Indianapolis, IN, 1987.

"The Plan to Steal Your 401(k)," http://www.rushlimbaugh.com/daily/2012/11/29/details_the_plan_to_steal_your_401_k, 2012.

"The 401(k) Confiscation: The Ghilarducci Plan," http://www.nc renegade.com/editorial/the-401k-confiscation-the-ghilarducci-plan-ann-barnhardt/, 2012.

"Thirteen American Cities Going Broke," 247Alex, http://www.247wallst.com, 10/25/12.

Washingtons Blog, "The Myth That U.S. Has Never Defaulted On Its Debt," http://www.ritholtz.com/blog/2013/10/the-myth-that-u-s-has-never-defaulted-on-its-debt/, 2013.

Worsley, F. A., *Endurance*, W.W. Norton and Co., New York, NY, 2000.

Young, Fred J., *How To Get Rich and Stay Rich*, Lifetime Periodicals, Hollywood, FL, 1996.

Zitz, Michael, *Giving It All Away: The Doris Buffet Story*, The Permanent Press, Sag Harbor, NY, 2010.

Zuccaro, Robert, *Dow 30,000 by 2008!: Why It's Different this Time*, Palisade Press, Jersey City, NJ, 2003.

Zweig, Jason, *Our Government Bonds? Here's Why You Should Be Worried*, http://www.online.wsj.com. 2011.

Index

CPSIA information can be obtained at www.ICGtesting.com
Printed in the USA
LVOW13*0710230814

400370LV00001B/3/P